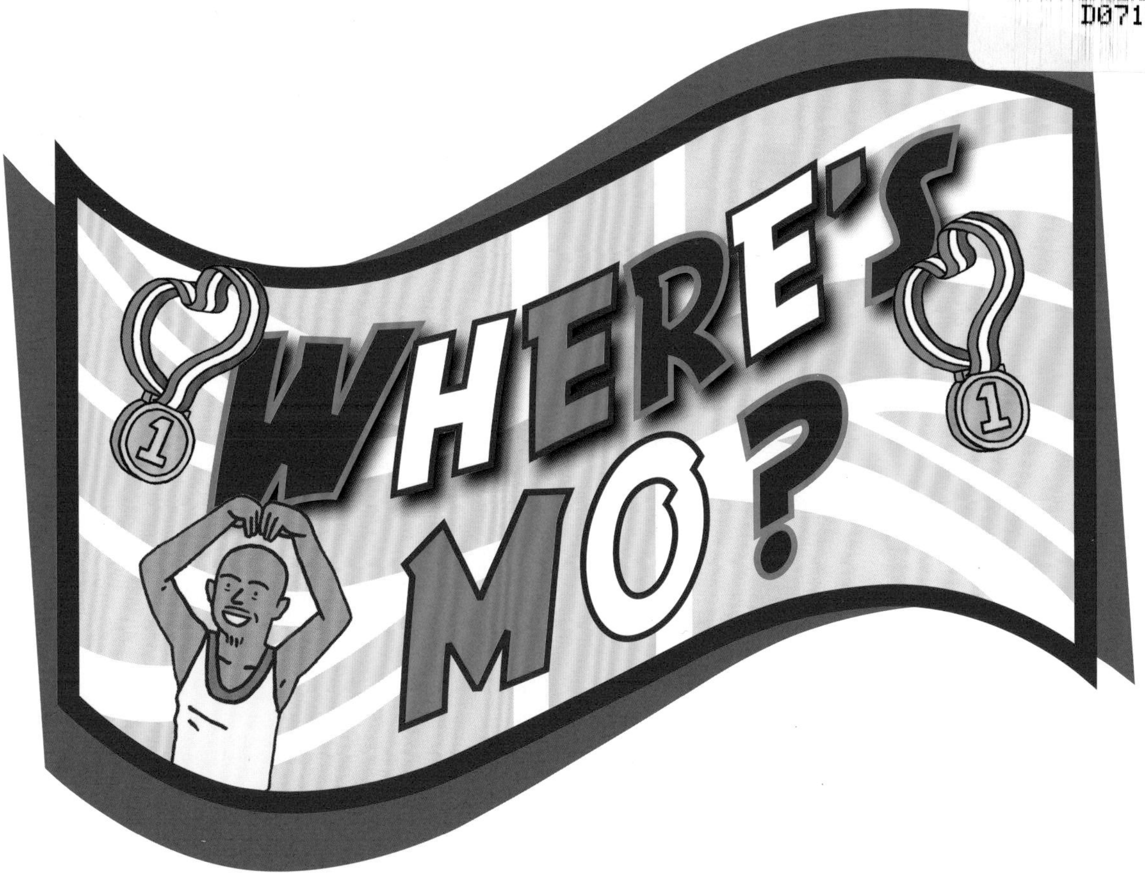
WHERE'S MO?
1
1

FIND MO FARAH AND HIS SPORTING FRIENDS IN 15 FUN-FILLED PUZZLES

ILLUSTRATED BY HARRY BLOOM
WORDS BY SARA CYWINSKI
DESIGNED BY GRAEME ANDREW

JB
JOHN BLAKE

Published by John Blake Publishing Ltd,
3 Bramber Court, 2 Bramber Road,
London W14 9PB, England

www.johnblakepublishing.co.uk

www.facebook.com/Johnblakepub
twitter.com/johnblakepub

First published in hardback in 2012

ISBN: 978 1 78219 071 4

British Library Cataloguing-in-Publication Data:

A catalogue record for this book is available from the British Library.

Designed by www.envydesign.co.uk
Printed and bound in the UK by Butler Tanner & Dennis Ltd., Frome, Somerset.

1 3 5 7 9 10 8 6 4 2

Papers used by John Blake Publishing are natural, recyclable products made from wood grown in sustainable forests. The manufacturing processes conform to the environmental regulations of the country of origin.

Every attempt has been made to contact the relevant copyright-holders, but some were unobtainable. We would be grateful if the appropriate people could contact us.

MO'S MISSION

Hello friends!

I've just finished running 5,000m and 10,000m in London. I represent Great Britain, and I really love sport. I've made it my mission to travel all over the country (and beyond) supporting fellow athletes as they compete against each other. It's going to be really exciting!

I didn't want to go on this adventure alone because that wouldn't be fun. I've decided to ask four friends to join me. Guess who has agreed to come with me... diver Tom Daley, horse rider Zara Phillips, cyclist Bradley Wiggins and heptathlon champion Jessica Ennis. You can come, too, if you like! It's going to be fun. The only catch is you'll have to find me first!

All the sporting events we are attending are exceptionally busy and popular, so you're going to have to use your sharp eyes and searching skills to spot me in the crowds. Oh, and I forgot to mention, all my friends are hiding too.

I haven't made it easy for you, either. In each sporting event, there are 10 other things you have to find. I've included a checklist, so you can tick each thing off after you have found it. There is a gold medal to be found, too, as a reward for all your hard work! Shabba!

Good luck.

PS. If you get stuck, the answers can be found in the back of the book.

MEET MO

Mo Farah is Britain's finest male long-distance runner of his generation. He was born in Somalia but moved to the UK when he was around eight years old. Mo loves running, but when he was younger he really loved football. His favourite football team is Arsenal. His favourite athletic hero was British 400m runner Jamie Baulch. Mo used to bleach his hair to look like Jamie. When Mo isn't running he likes listening to music on his i-Pod, but when Mo is in training he runs about 20 miles! Crikey!

Mo is the current 10,000m Olympic champion and 5,000m Olympic, World and European champion, making him the world's fastest long-distance runner. In the 2012 Olympic Games, Mo was the first athlete to win gold for Great Britain in the 10,000m.

Mo's favourite signature move is the 'Mobot'. He's always striking the pose, so if you're hoping to find Mo super fast in the puzzles to follow – keep an eye out for the Mobot!

SPORTING FIGURES

Find out more about Mo's friends here. And discover what they look like, so you can find them quicker!

JESSICA ENNIS

Jess is the current Olympic heptathlon champion. This means she competed in seven events! The events included: 100m hurdles, high jump, shot put, 200m, long jump, javelin and 800m. Jess started training when she was just 11 years old. When she isn't competing or training, Jess loves watching television programmes. She is a fan of Sheffield United Football Club.

BRADLEY WIGGINS

Bradley loves cycling! He is a British professional track and road racing cyclist. He started his career on the track, like Sir Chris Hoy, but moved on to road racing. Bradley won the exceptionally difficult Tour de France race in 2012, as well as a gold medal in the 2012 Olympic Games. When Bradley isn't cycling he likes to cheer on his football team, Liverpool FC. He also likes to collect scooters and guitars and he loves music.

TOM DALEY

Everybody loves Tom Daley! He is an English diver and specialises in the 10m platform event. Tom started diving when he was seven years old. He represented Britain in the 2008 Beijing Olympics and was the youngest competitor to take part. When Tom isn't diving or swimming in the pool, he likes to hang out with his friends!

ZARA PHILLIPS

Zara is the eldest granddaughter of the Queen! But that's not the only reason she is famous. Zara is a respected British equestrian, and she won a silver medal at the 2012 Olympic Games. She has also won gold medals in lots of other equestrian competitions, including the 2005 European Eventing Championship. Zara doesn't just love to ride horses; she represented her school in hockey, athletics and gymnastics.

A gold medal is normally awarded for the highest achievement in sport. Not all medals are made of solid gold. For example, the medals awarded to athletes in the 2012 Olympic Games were gold-plated. Olympic gold medals are required to be made from at least 92.5 per cent silver and they must contain 6 grams of gold! Every athlete strives to win a gold medal, including Mo Farah.

TRACK STADIUM

Mo and friends are in the stadium. Mo's running pal, Usain Bolt, is taking part in the 100m race. I wonder if he will get a new world record. Find Mo and his friends in 9.58 seconds to get the same time Usain Bolt took to run the 100m. On your marks, get set... GO!

Fun fact: The biggest stadium in the world is in North Korea. It's called the Rungrado May Day Stadium. It holds 150, 000 people.

CHECKLIST

- Usain Bolt
- A cheater
- A javelin
- Someone jumping over a hurdle
- Gold running shoes
- The winner's podium
- An ice-cream seller
- A girl with a balloon
- A starting pistol
- Boris Johnson and David Cameron dancing

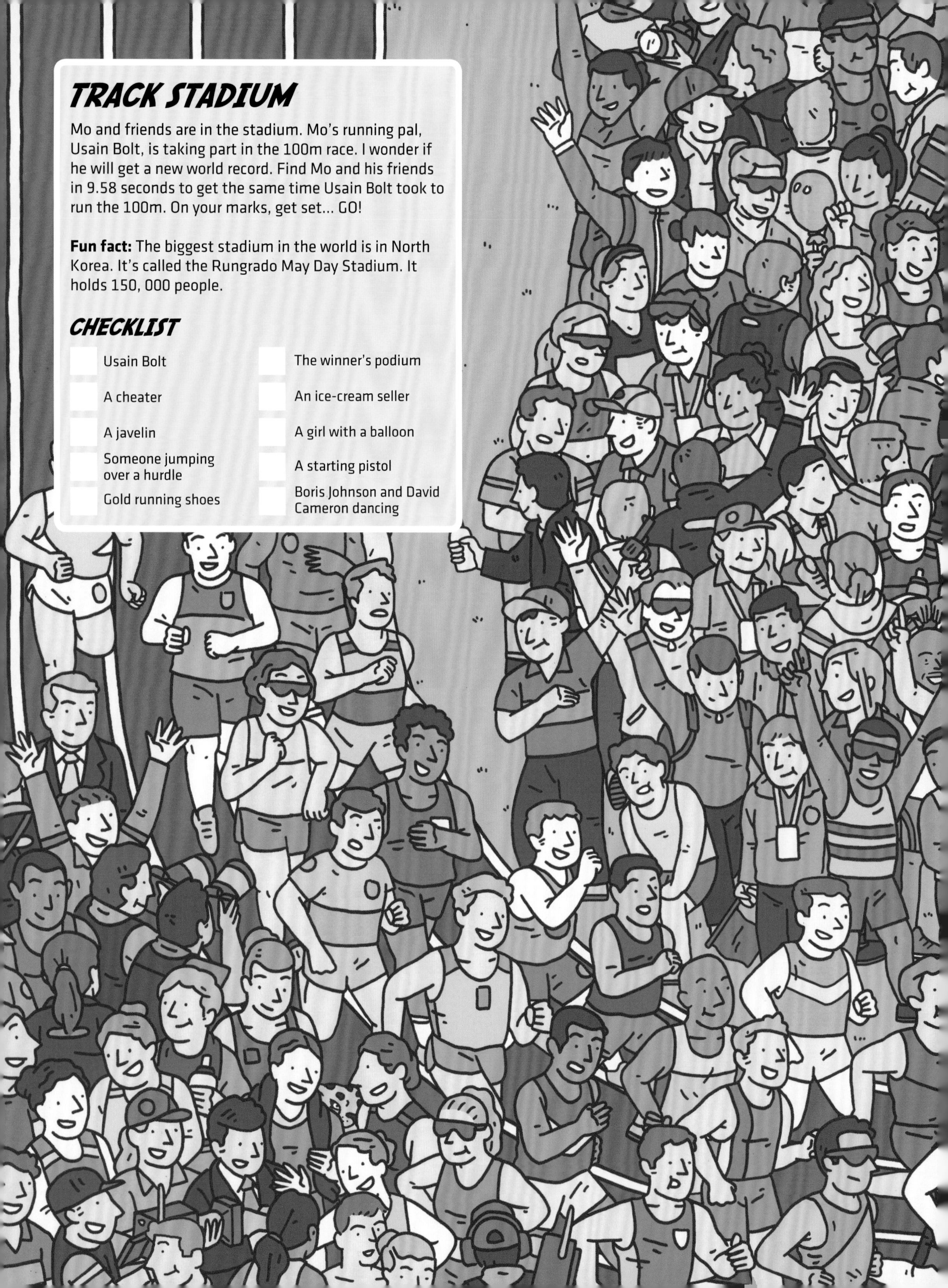

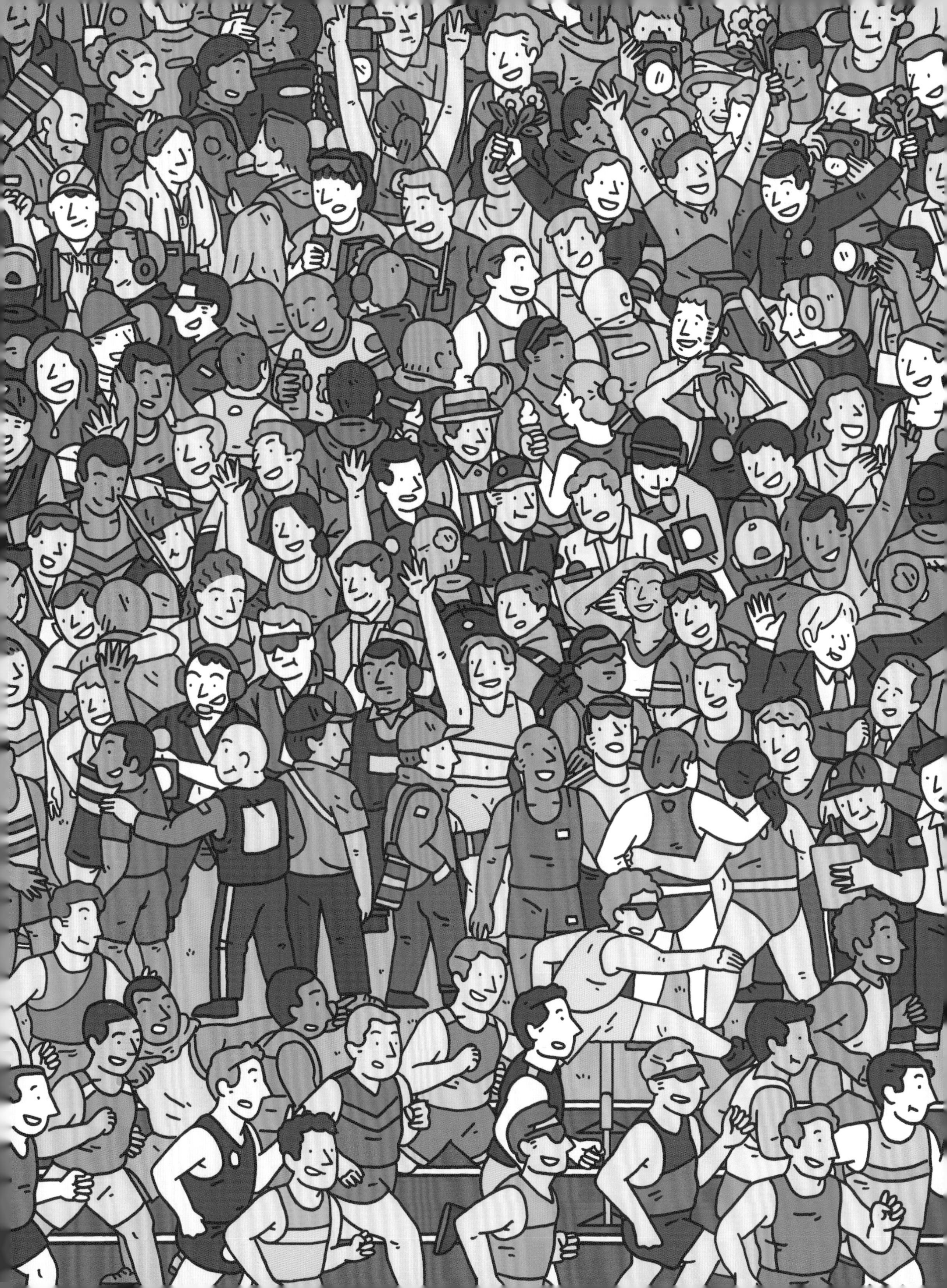

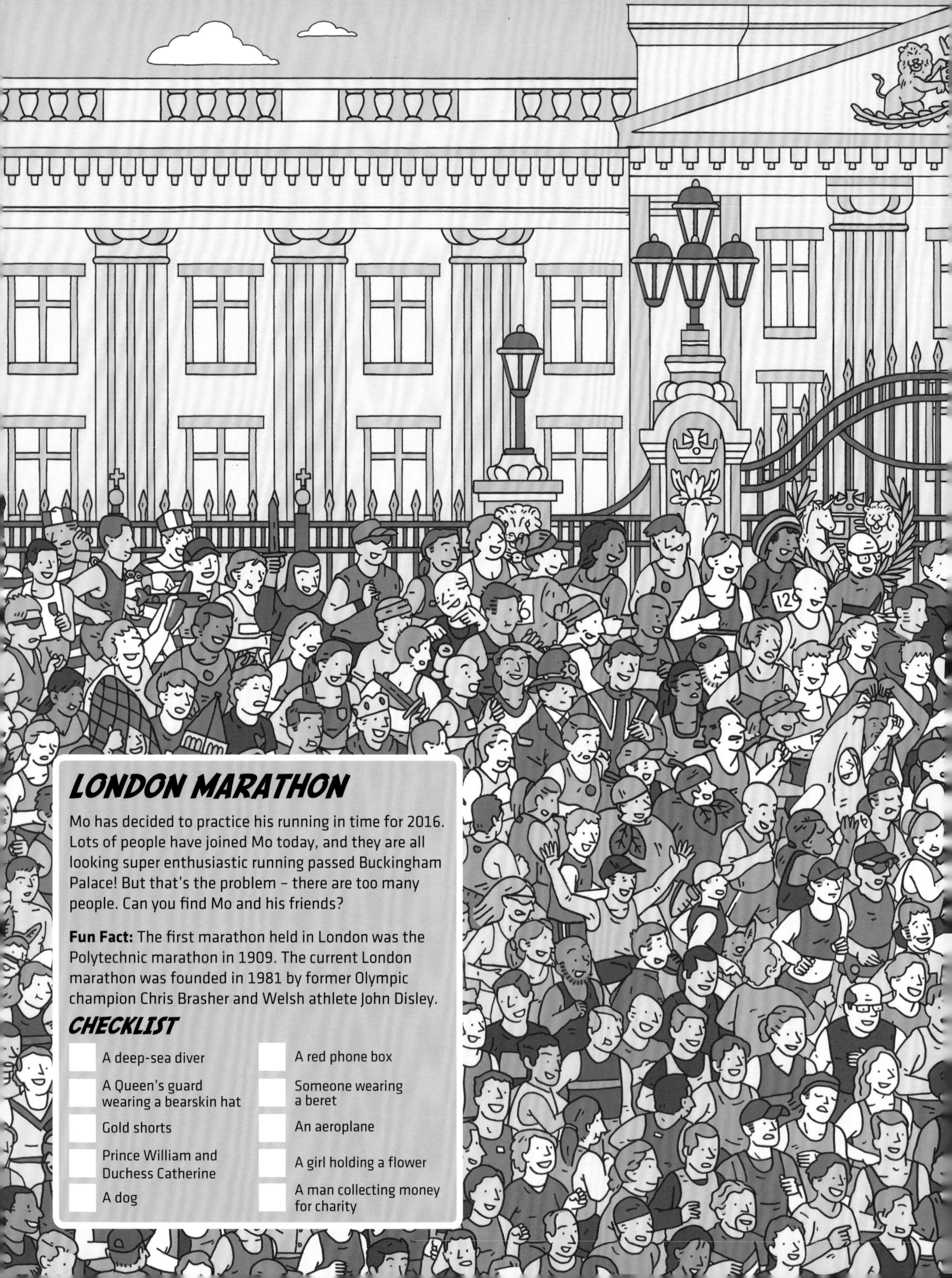

LONDON MARATHON

Mo has decided to practice his running in time for 2016. Lots of people have joined Mo today, and they are all looking super enthusiastic running passed Buckingham Palace! But that's the problem – there are too many people. Can you find Mo and his friends?

Fun Fact: The first marathon held in London was the Polytechnic marathon in 1909. The current London marathon was founded in 1981 by former Olympic champion Chris Brasher and Welsh athlete John Disley.

CHECKLIST

- [ ] A deep-sea diver
- [ ] A Queen's guard wearing a bearskin hat
- [ ] Gold shorts
- [ ] Prince William and Duchess Catherine
- [ ] A dog
- [ ] A red phone box
- [ ] Someone wearing a beret
- [ ] An aeroplane
- [ ] A girl holding a flower
- [ ] A man collecting money for charity

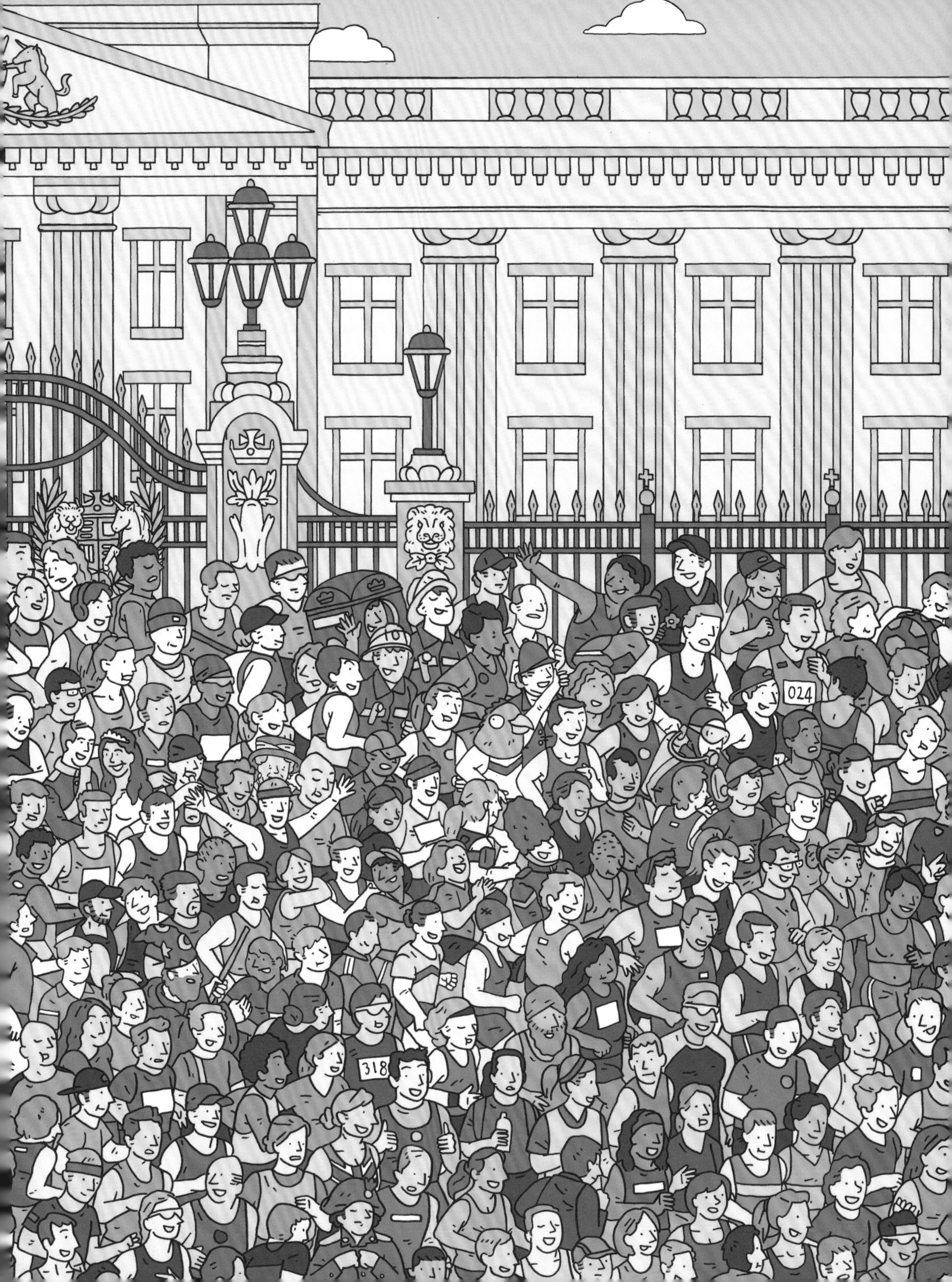
024
318

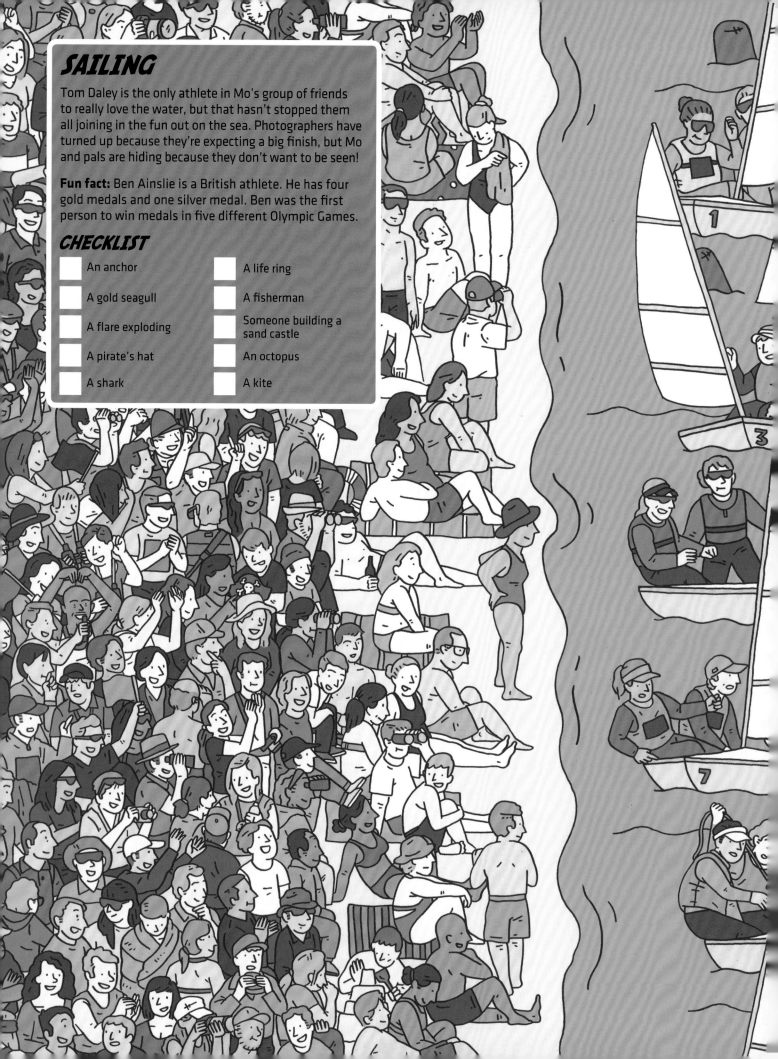

SAILING

Tom Daley is the only athlete in Mo's group of friends to really love the water, but that hasn't stopped them all joining in the fun out on the sea. Photographers have turned up because they're expecting a big finish, but Mo and pals are hiding because they don't want to be seen!

Fun fact: Ben Ainslie is a British athlete. He has four gold medals and one silver medal. Ben was the first person to win medals in five different Olympic Games.

CHECKLIST

- [ ] An anchor
- [ ] A gold seagull
- [ ] A flare exploding
- [ ] A pirate's hat
- [ ] A shark
- [ ] A life ring
- [ ] A fisherman
- [ ] Someone building a sand castle
- [ ] An octopus
- [ ] A kite

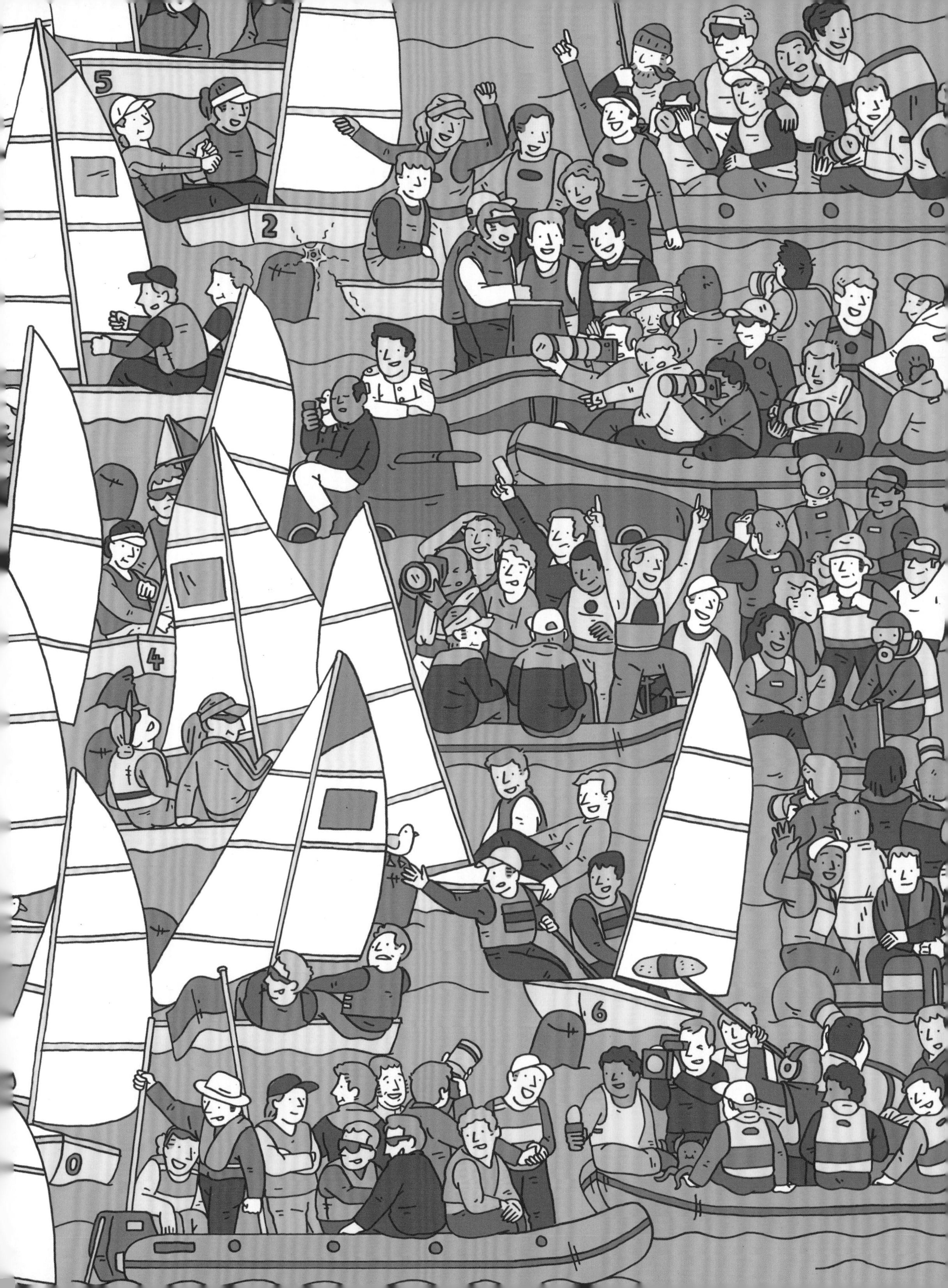
5
2
4
6
0

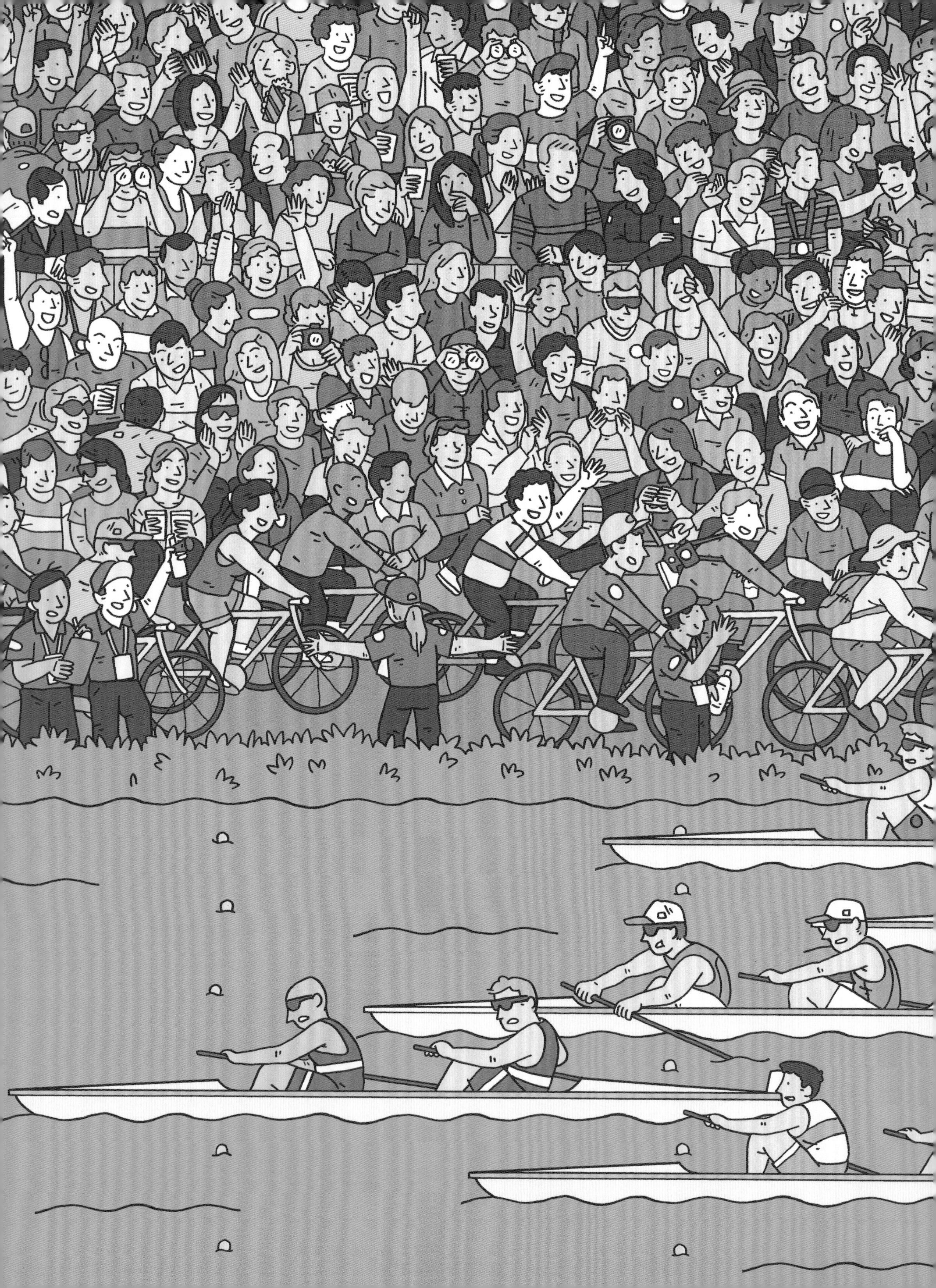

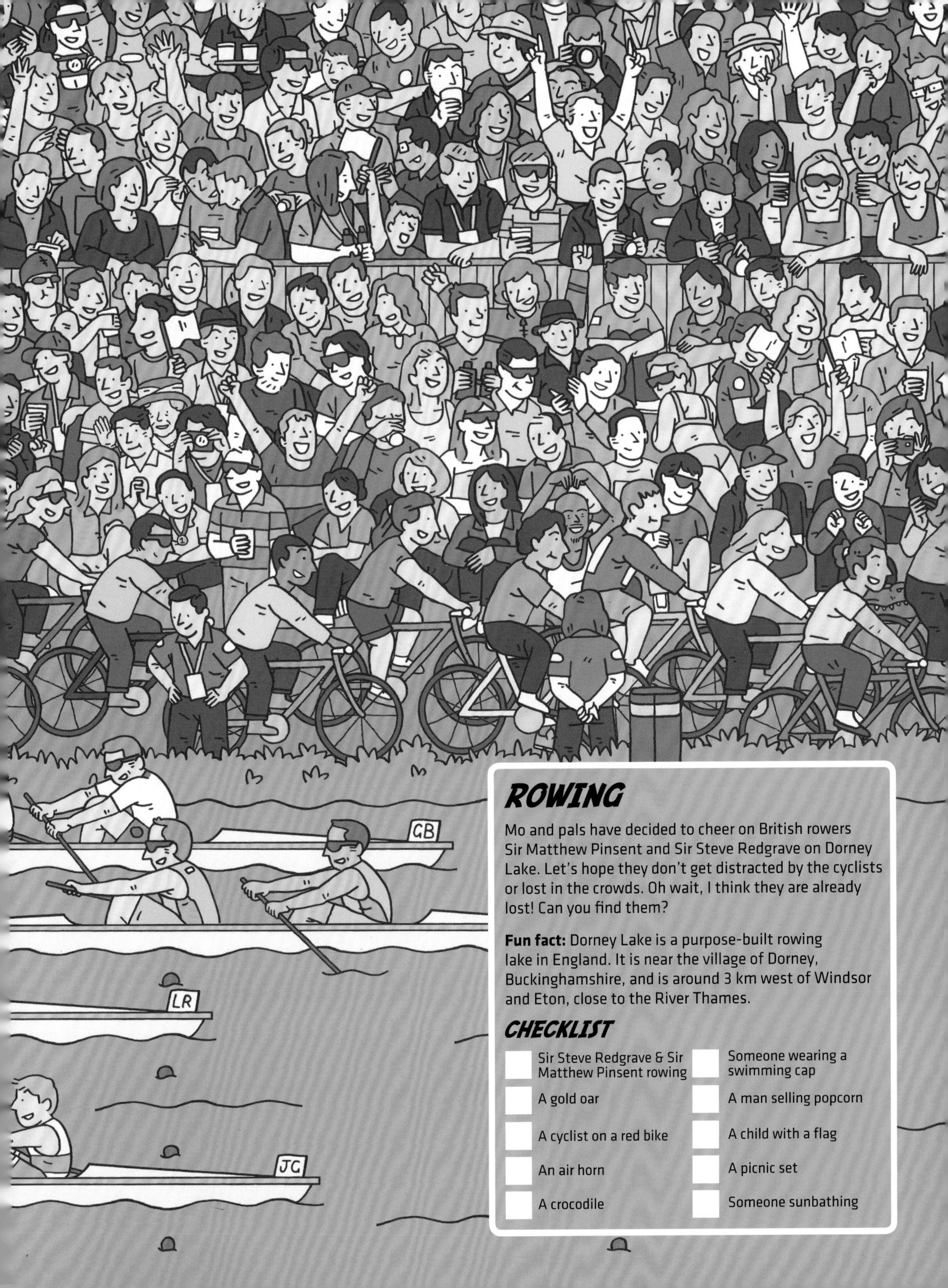
GB
LR
JG

ROWING

Mo and pals have decided to cheer on British rowers Sir Matthew Pinsent and Sir Steve Redgrave on Dorney Lake. Let's hope they don't get distracted by the cyclists or lost in the crowds. Oh wait, I think they are already lost! Can you find them?

Fun fact: Dorney Lake is a purpose-built rowing lake in England. It is near the village of Dorney, Buckinghamshire, and is around 3 km west of Windsor and Eton, close to the River Thames.

CHECKLIST

- [ ] Sir Steve Redgrave & Sir Matthew Pinsent rowing
- [ ] A gold oar
- [ ] A cyclist on a red bike
- [ ] An air horn
- [ ] A crocodile
- [ ] Someone wearing a swimming cap
- [ ] A man selling popcorn
- [ ] A child with a flag
- [ ] A picnic set
- [ ] Someone sunbathing

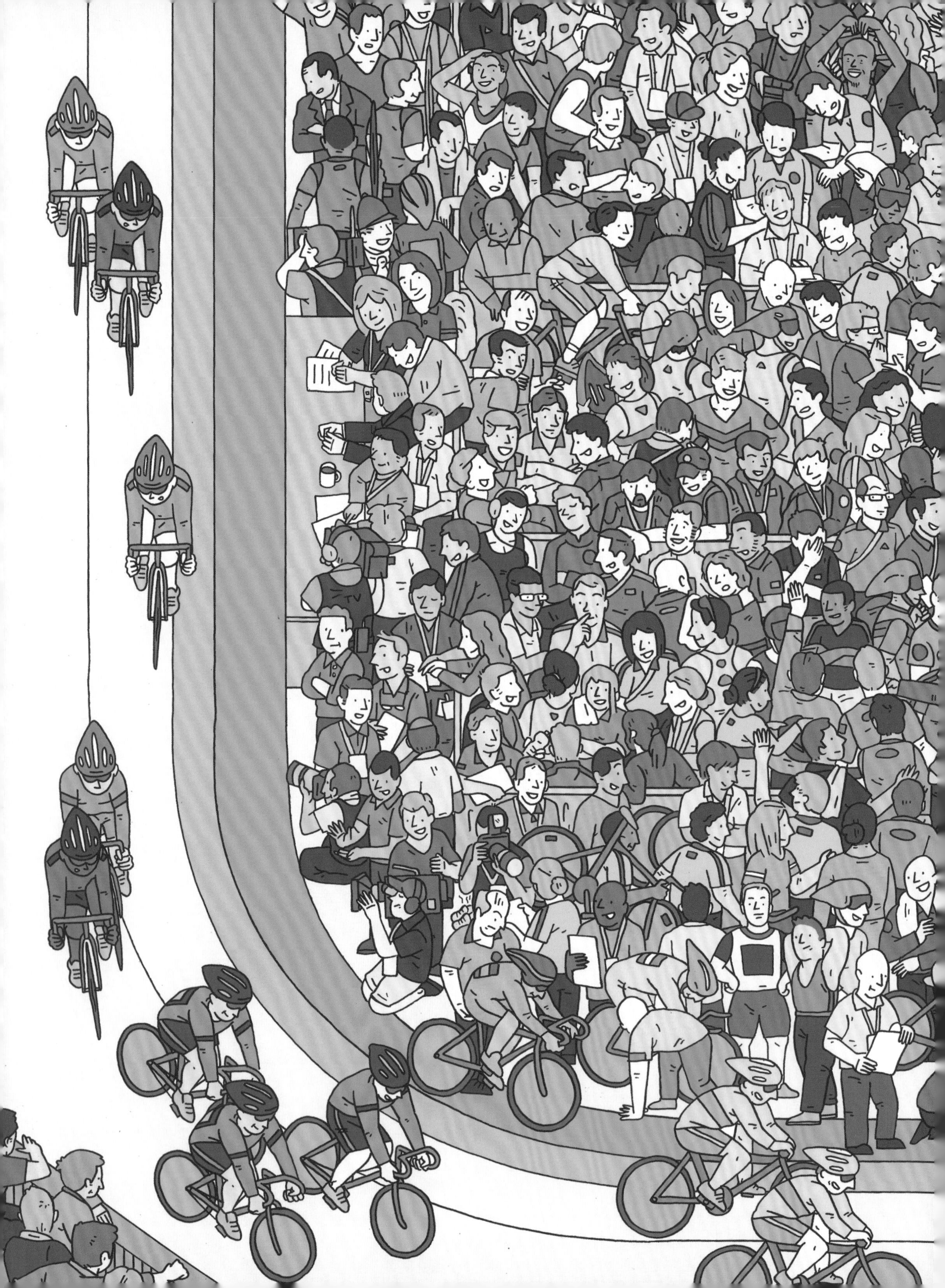
TV

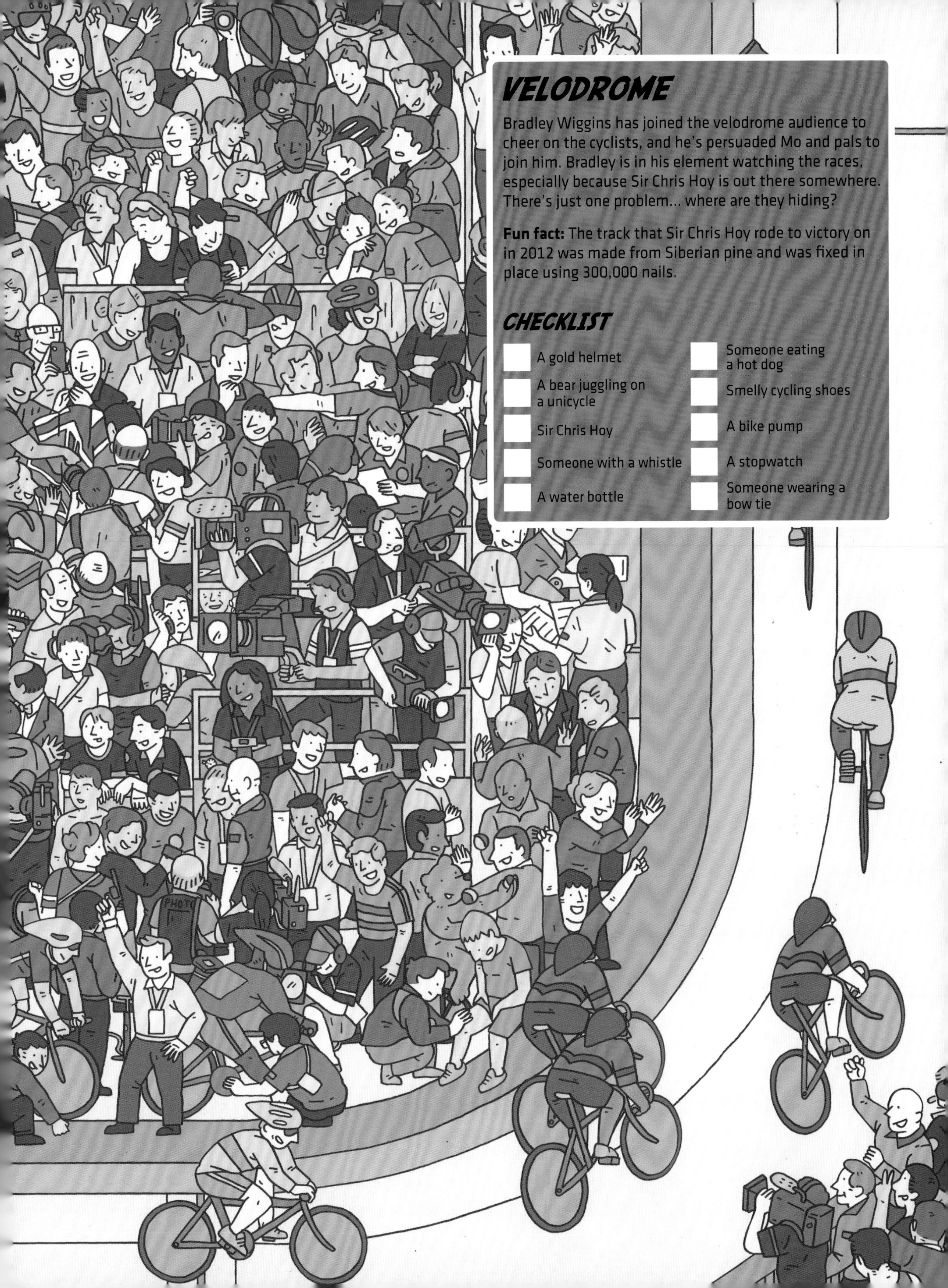
PHOTO

VELODROME

Bradley Wiggins has joined the velodrome audience to cheer on the cyclists, and he's persuaded Mo and pals to join him. Bradley is in his element watching the races, especially because Sir Chris Hoy is out there somewhere. There's just one problem... where are they hiding?

Fun fact: The track that Sir Chris Hoy rode to victory on in 2012 was made from Siberian pine and was fixed in place using 300,000 nails.

CHECKLIST

- [ ] A gold helmet
- [ ] A bear juggling on a unicycle
- [ ] Sir Chris Hoy
- [ ] Someone with a whistle
- [ ] A water bottle
- [ ] Someone eating a hot dog
- [ ] Smelly cycling shoes
- [ ] A bike pump
- [ ] A stopwatch
- [ ] Someone wearing a bow tie

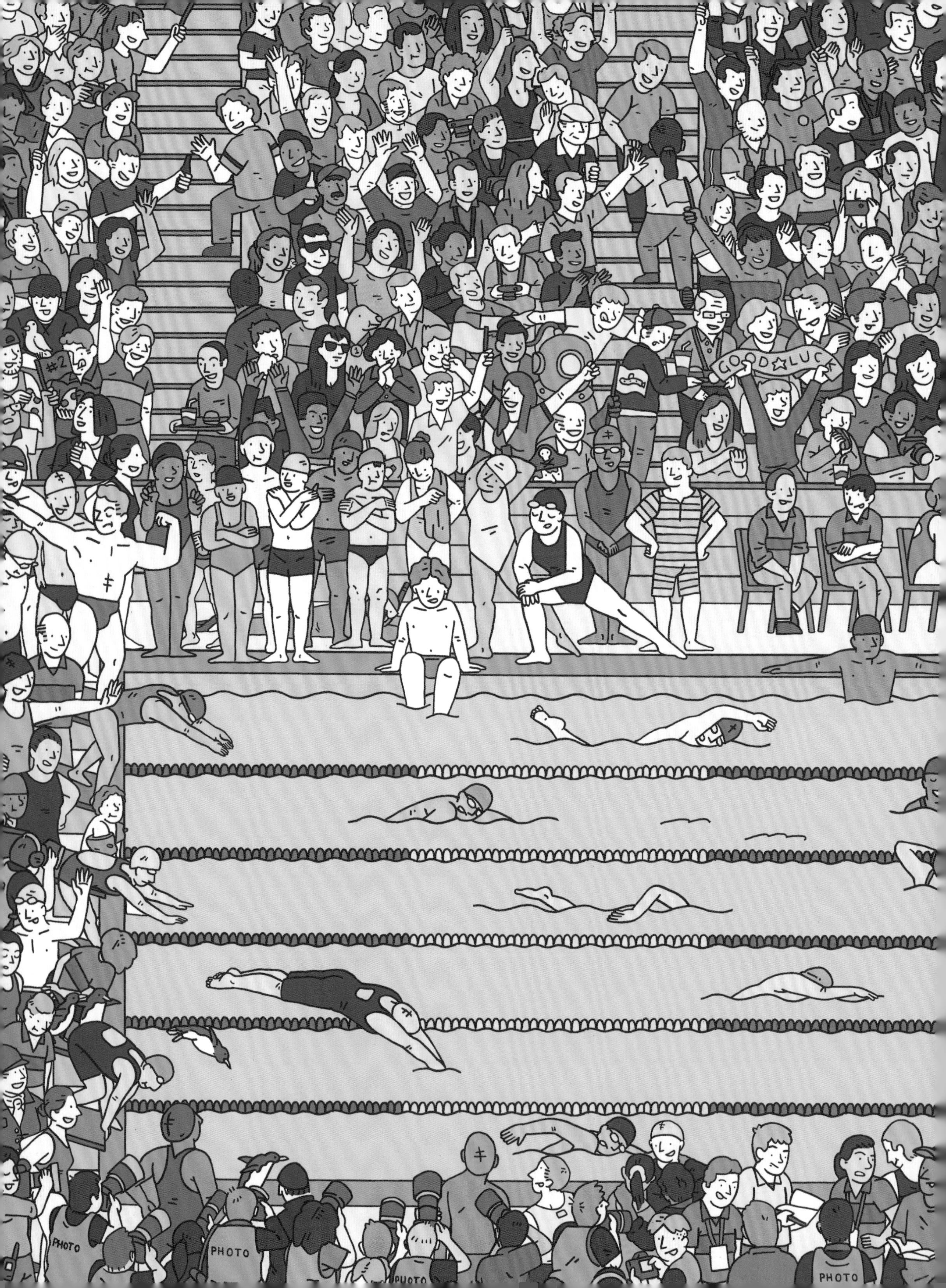
GOOD☆LUCK
#2
PHOTO
PHOTO
PHOTO
PHOTO

SWIMMING POOL

Tom loves diving! Mo, Jess, Zara and Bradley have joined him in the pool to watch the synchronised swimmers, the diving experts and the super quick swimmers compete. The pool is very busy because everybody's going for gold. Can you find Mo and his pals?

Fun fact: The world's largest swimming pool can be found in Chile. It holds 66 million gallons of water. The length is 3323ft. It's said that the swimming pool cost £1 billion to build.

CHECKLIST

- [ ] A wet suit and snorkel
- [ ] A penguin diving
- [ ] Gold goggles
- [ ] A red diving board
- [ ] A green towel
- [ ] A beach ball
- [ ] A rubber duck
- [ ] A lifeguard
- [ ] A pink lilo
- [ ] A child wearing armbands

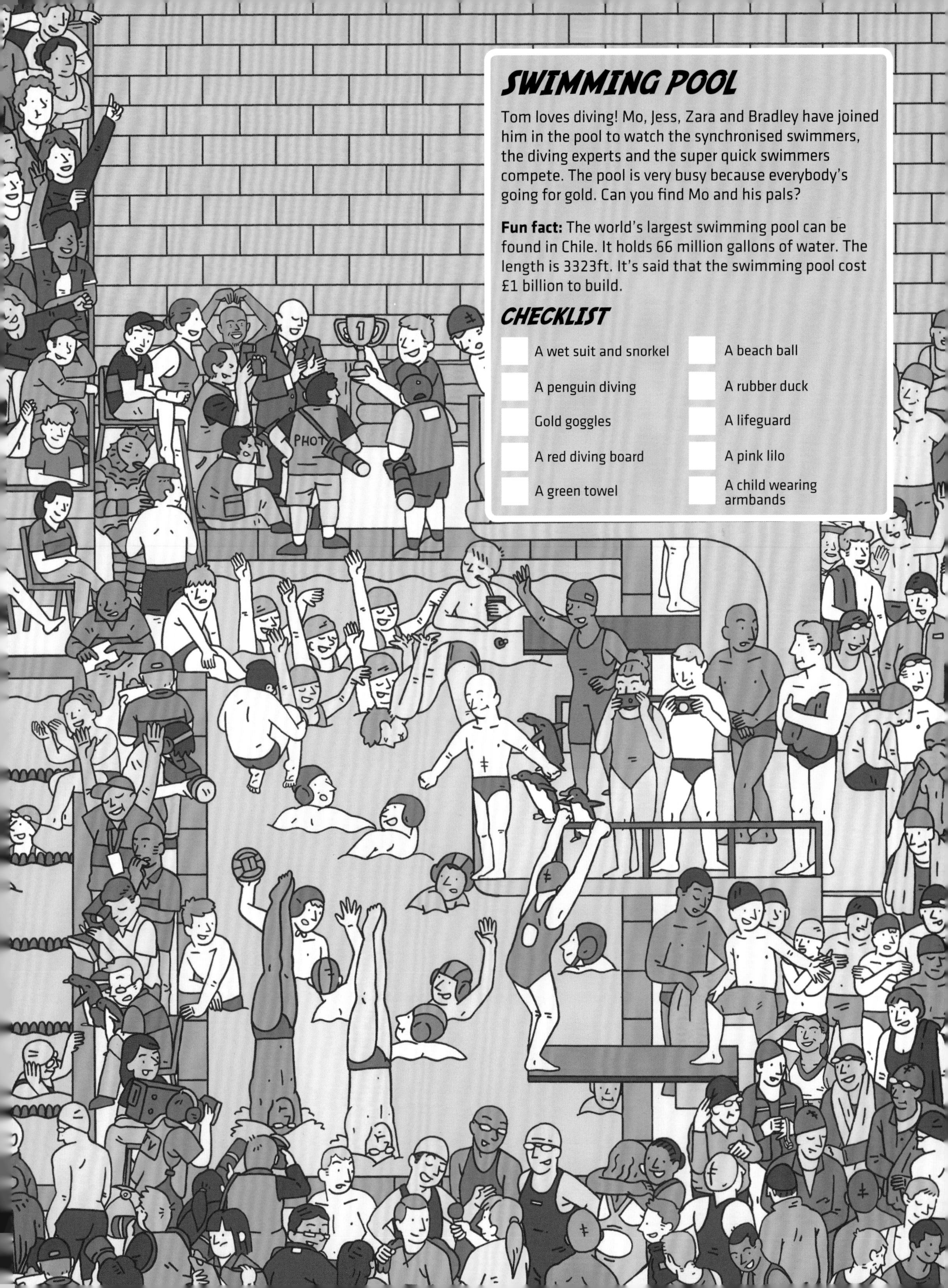
PHOT

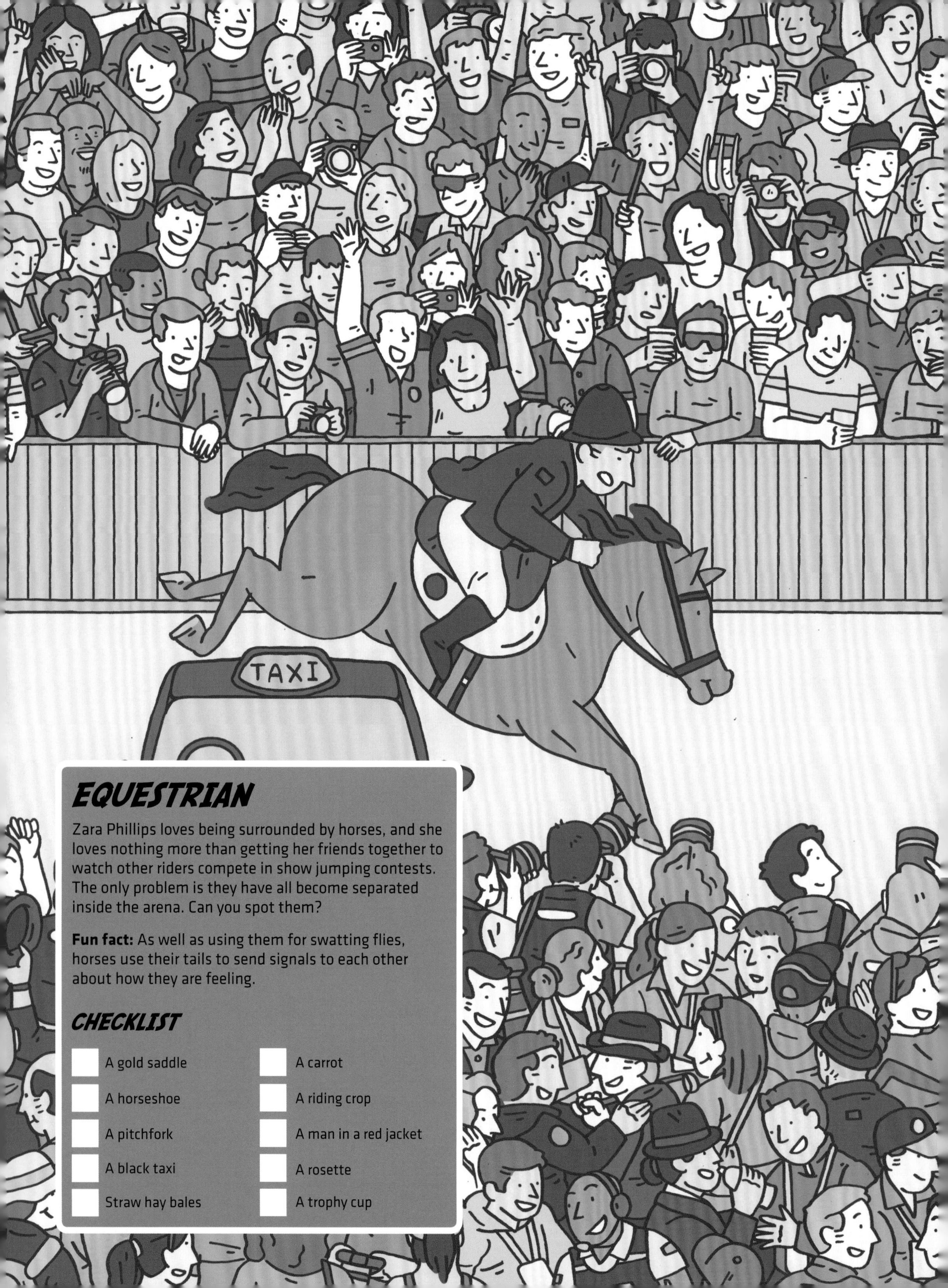
TAXI

EQUESTRIAN

Zara Phillips loves being surrounded by horses, and she loves nothing more than getting her friends together to watch other riders compete in show jumping contests. The only problem is they have all become separated inside the arena. Can you spot them?

Fun fact: As well as using them for swatting flies, horses use their tails to send signals to each other about how they are feeling.

CHECKLIST

- [ ] A gold saddle
- [ ] A horseshoe
- [ ] A pitchfork
- [ ] A black taxi
- [ ] Straw hay bales
- [ ] A carrot
- [ ] A riding crop
- [ ] A man in a red jacket
- [ ] A rosette
- [ ] A trophy cup

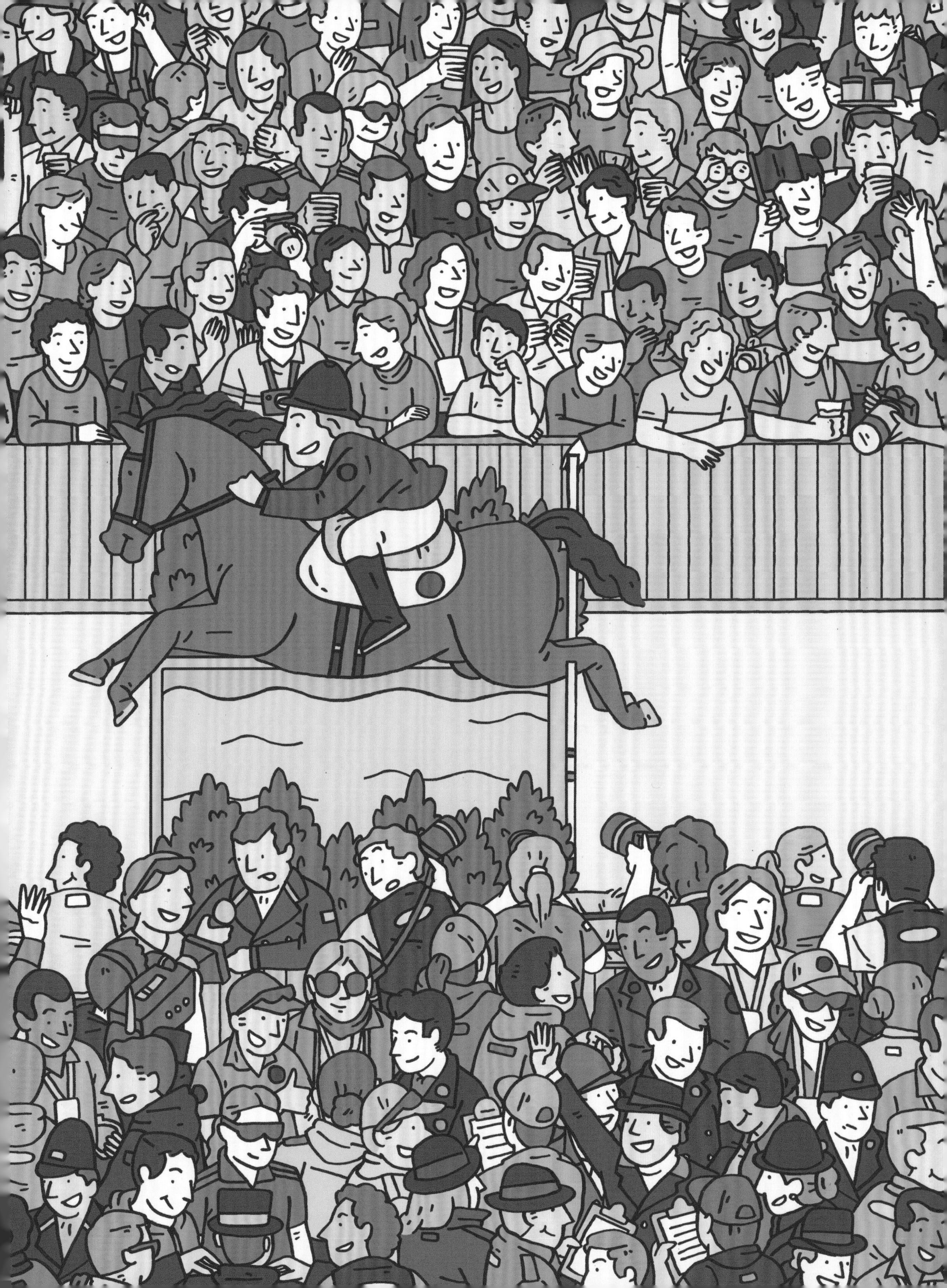

CYCLE ROAD RACE

UK road race cyclist Bradley Wiggins can't get enough of the cycling events, even if he isn't competing. He's joined Mo, Tom, Jess and Zara to support the amateur cyclists outside Hampton Court! Hampton Court is said to be haunted, and it would appear some ghostly beings have managed to separate Mo from his friends. Where have they gone?

Fun fact: Women started competing in the cycle road race in Los Angeles in 1984.

CHECKLIST

- [ ] A man on a bike wearing a yellow jersey
- [ ] A ghost
- [ ] Henry VIII
- [ ] A bike with training wheels
- [ ] A set of traffic lights
- [ ] A badger
- [ ] A bat
- [ ] A red car
- [ ] Someone eating a donut
- [ ] A police officer

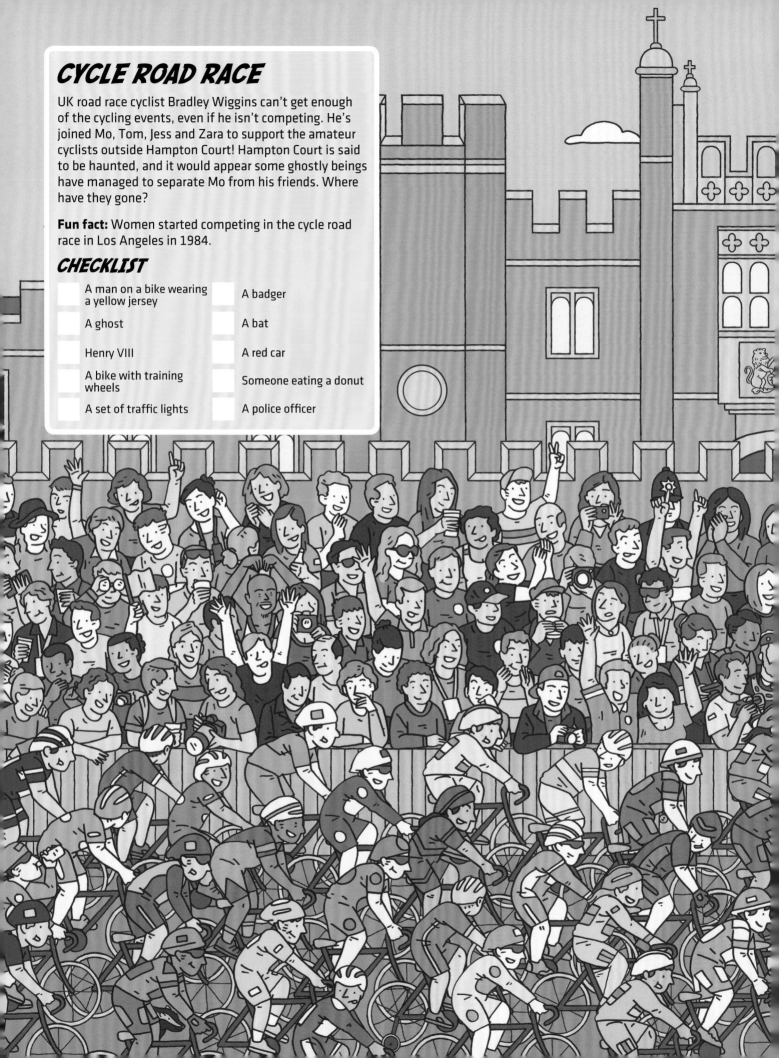

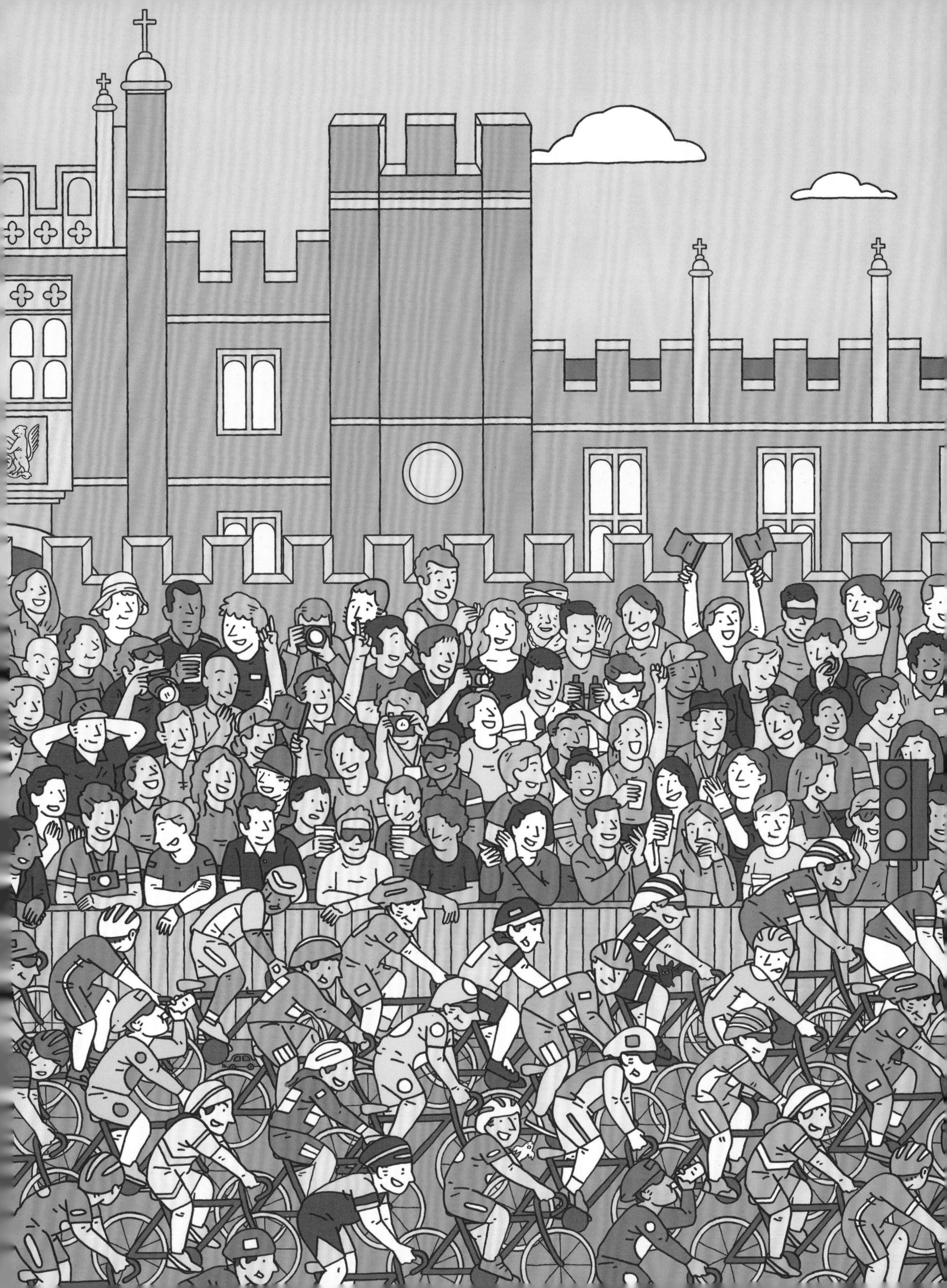

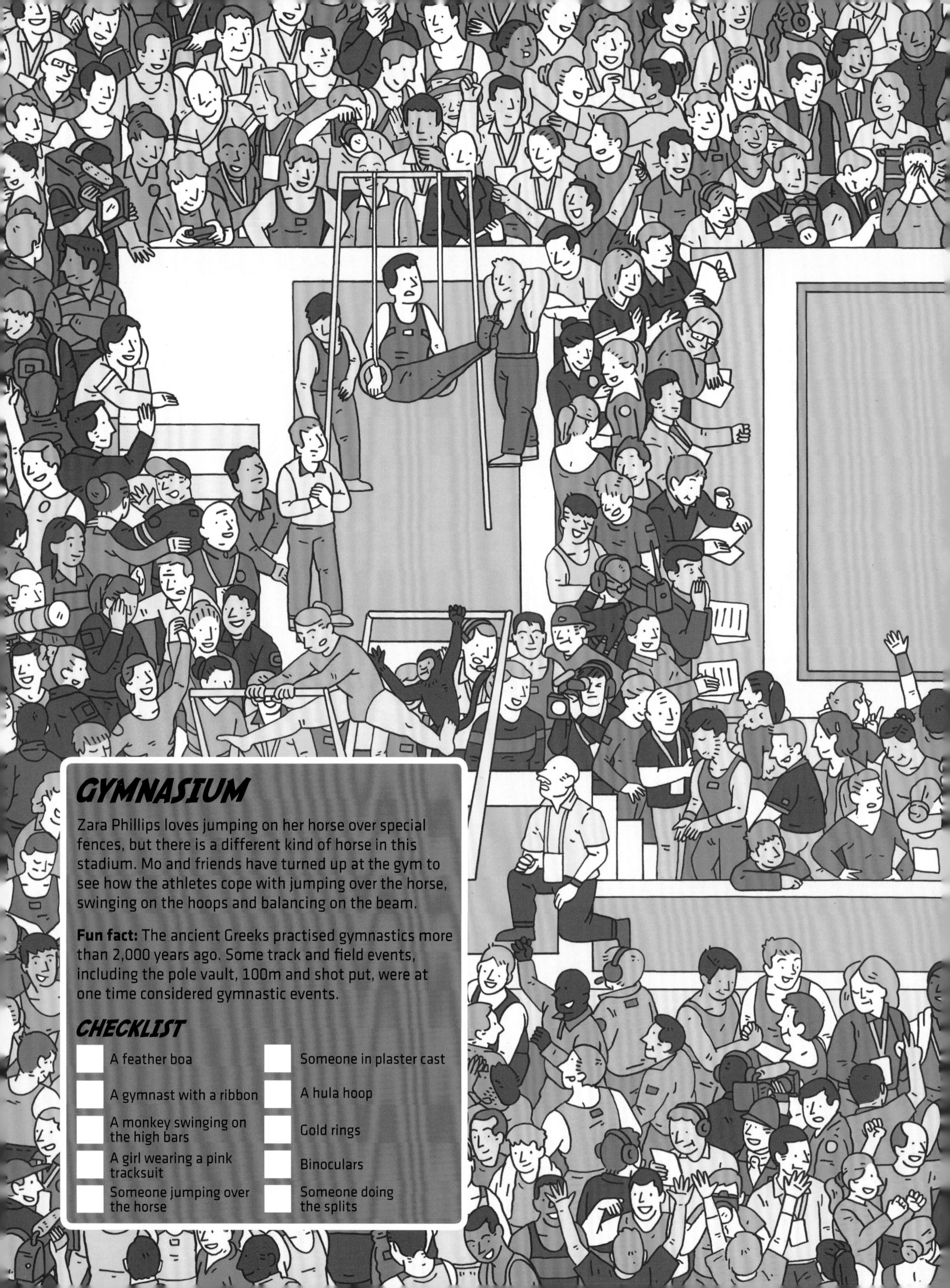

GYMNASIUM

Zara Phillips loves jumping on her horse over special fences, but there is a different kind of horse in this stadium. Mo and friends have turned up at the gym to see how the athletes cope with jumping over the horse, swinging on the hoops and balancing on the beam.

Fun fact: The ancient Greeks practised gymnastics more than 2,000 years ago. Some track and field events, including the pole vault, 100m and shot put, were at one time considered gymnastic events.

CHECKLIST

- [ ] A feather boa
- [ ] A gymnast with a ribbon
- [ ] A monkey swinging on the high bars
- [ ] A girl wearing a pink tracksuit
- [ ] Someone jumping over the horse
- [ ] Someone in plaster cast
- [ ] A hula hoop
- [ ] Gold rings
- [ ] Binoculars
- [ ] Someone doing the splits

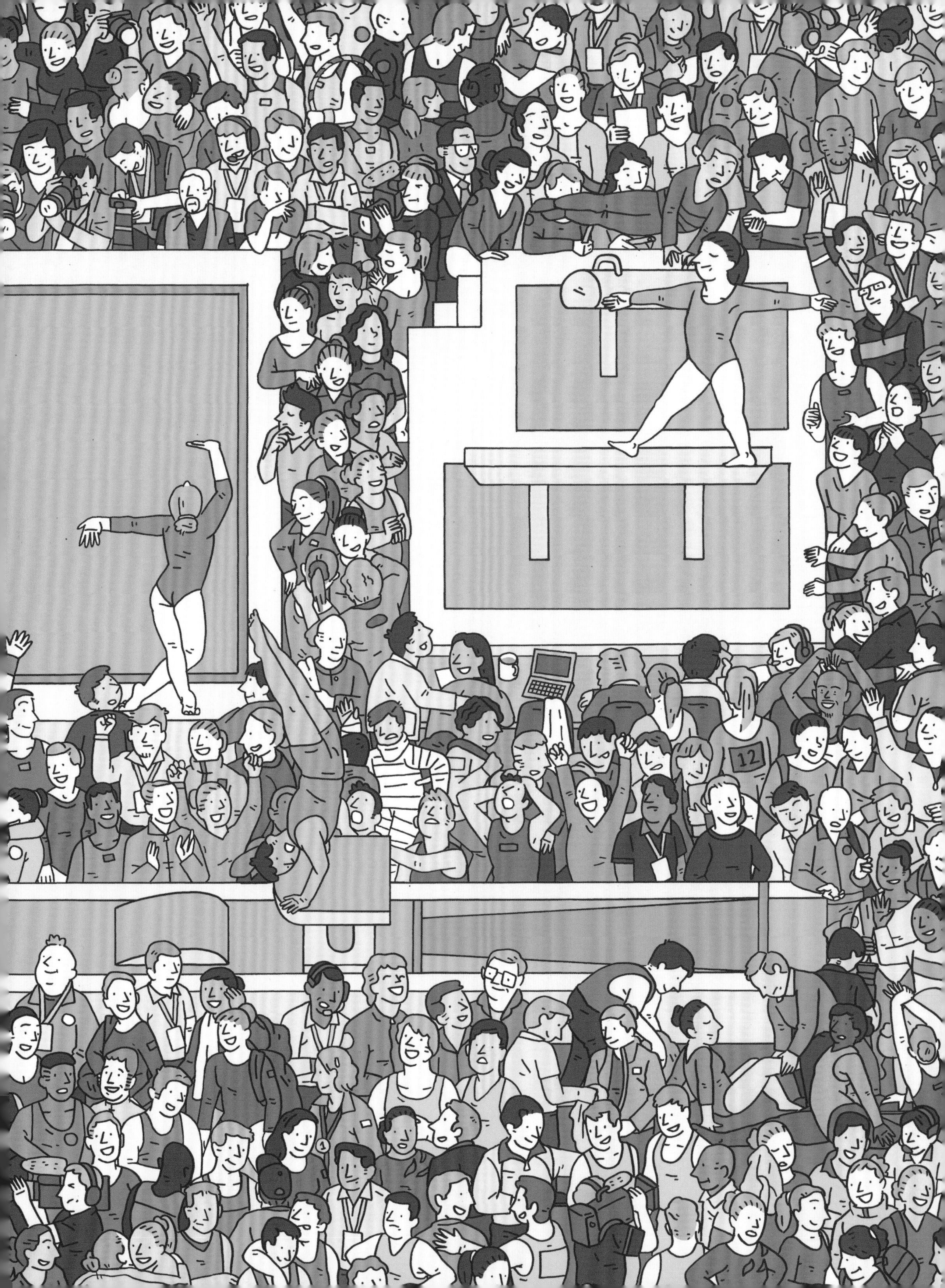
12

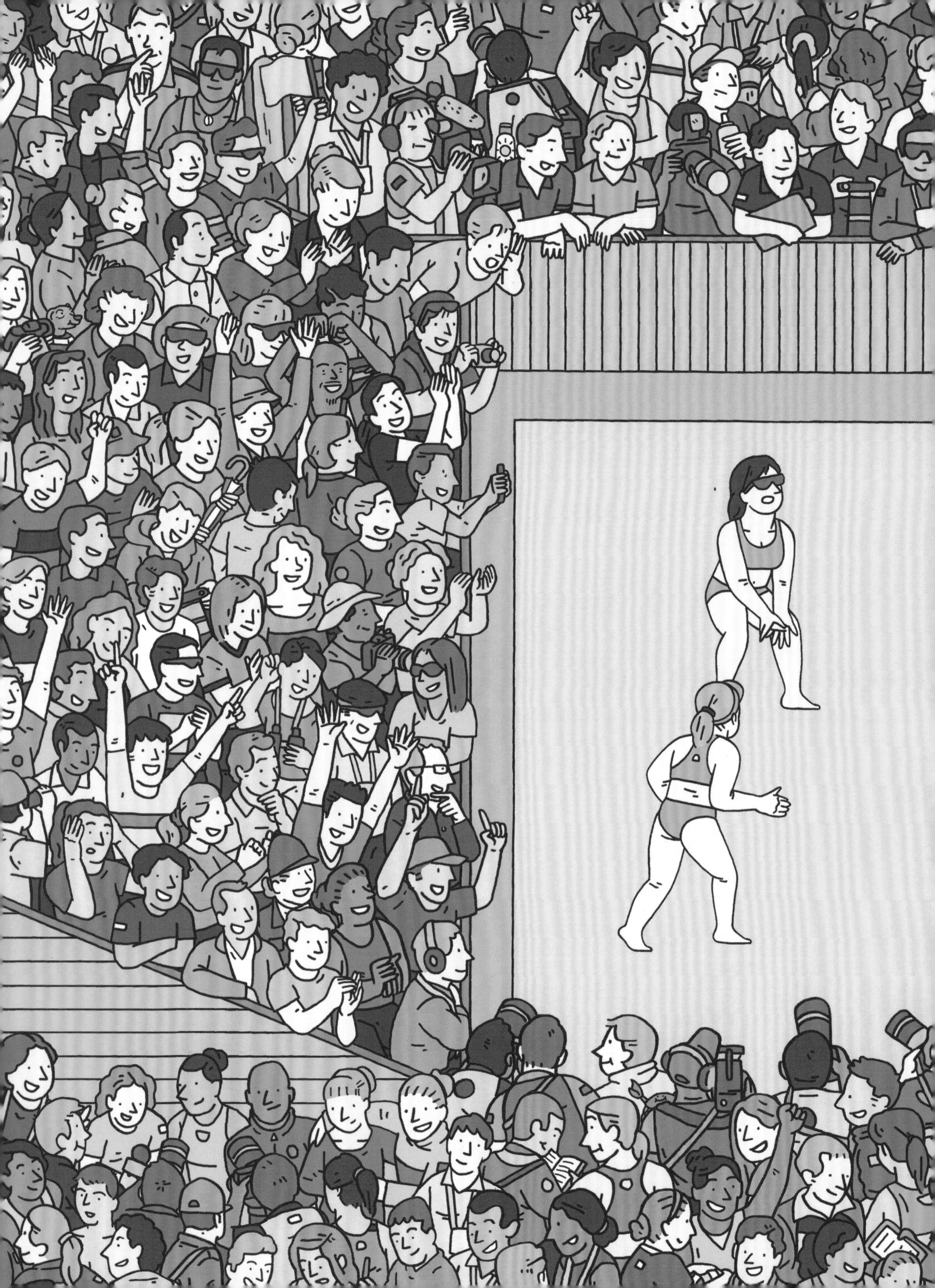

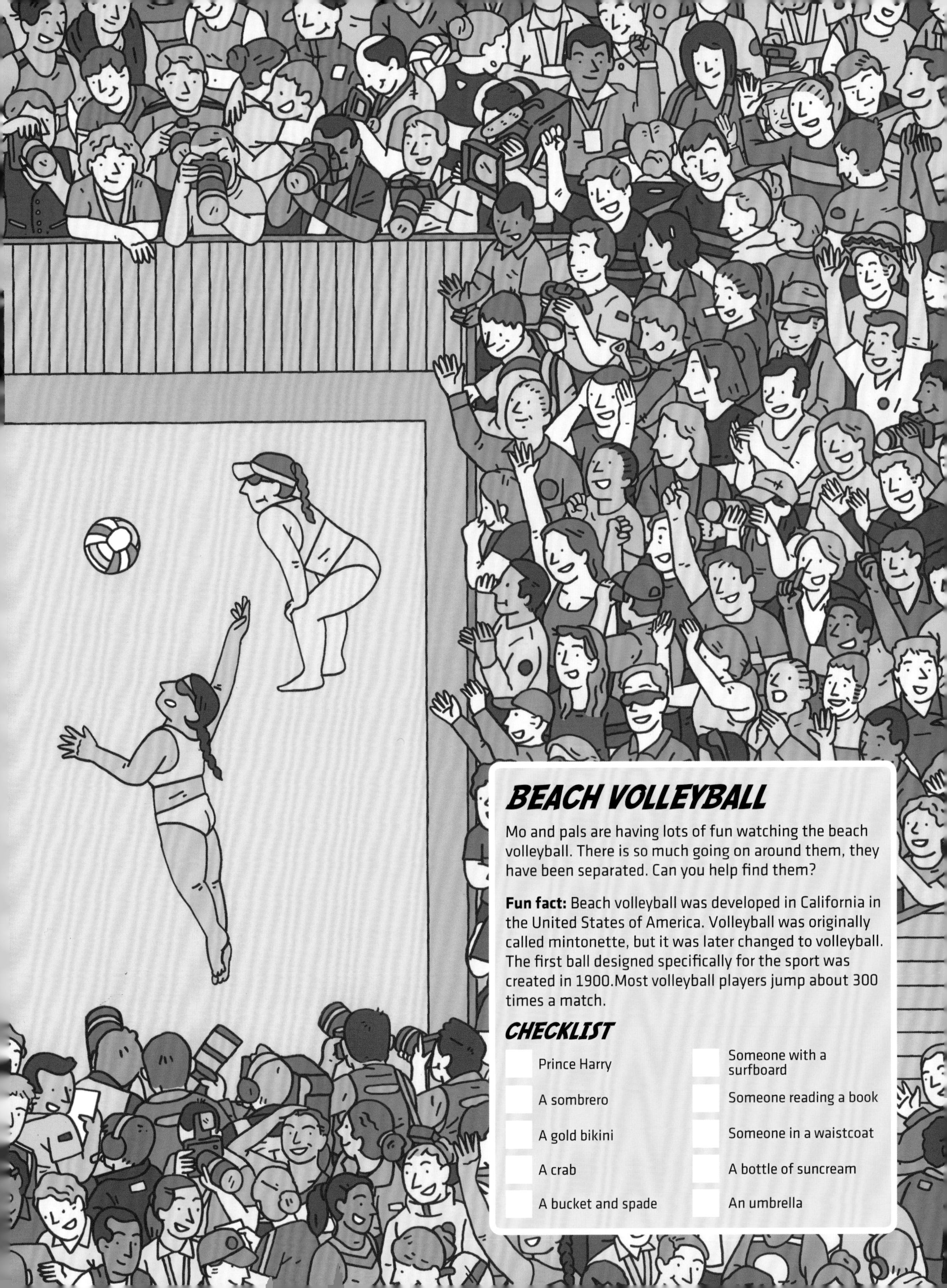

BEACH VOLLEYBALL

Mo and pals are having lots of fun watching the beach volleyball. There is so much going on around them, they have been separated. Can you help find them?

Fun fact: Beach volleyball was developed in California in the United States of America. Volleyball was originally called mintonette, but it was later changed to volleyball. The first ball designed specifically for the sport was created in 1900.Most volleyball players jump about 300 times a match.

CHECKLIST

- [ ] Prince Harry
- [ ] A sombrero
- [ ] A gold bikini
- [ ] A crab
- [ ] A bucket and spade
- [ ] Someone with a surfboard
- [ ] Someone reading a book
- [ ] Someone in a waistcoat
- [ ] A bottle of suncream
- [ ] An umbrella

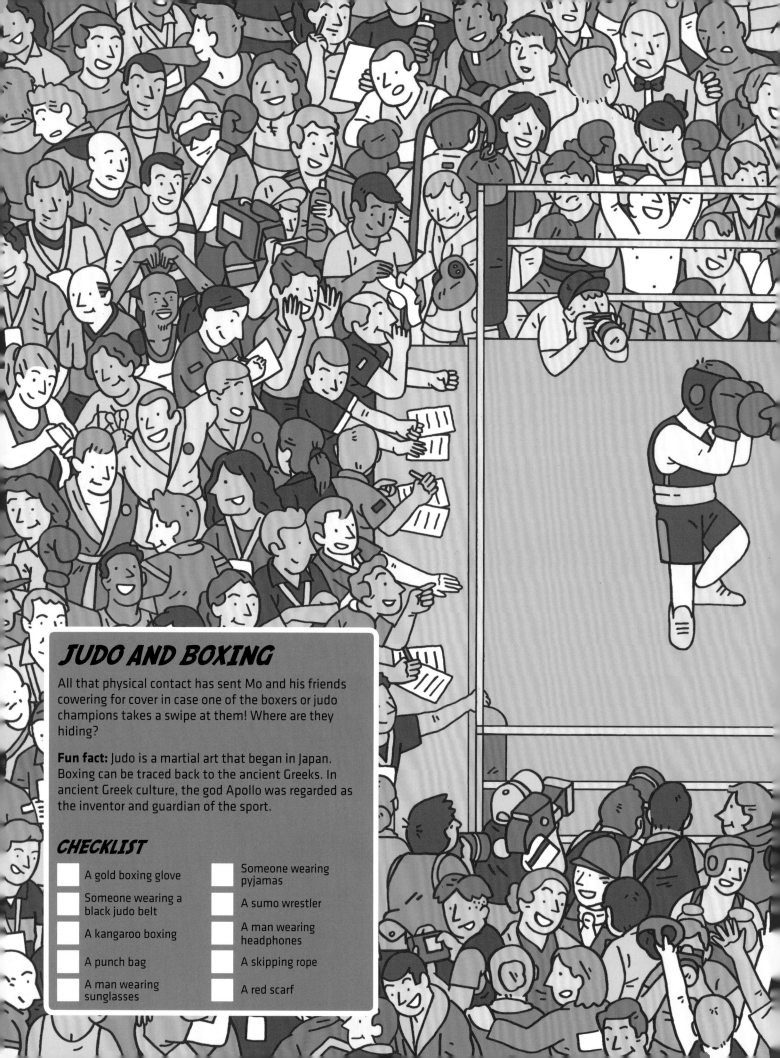

JUDO AND BOXING

All that physical contact has sent Mo and his friends cowering for cover in case one of the boxers or judo champions takes a swipe at them! Where are they hiding?

Fun fact: Judo is a martial art that began in Japan. Boxing can be traced back to the ancient Greeks. In ancient Greek culture, the god Apollo was regarded as the inventor and guardian of the sport.

CHECKLIST

- [ ] A gold boxing glove
- [ ] Someone wearing a black judo belt
- [ ] A kangaroo boxing
- [ ] A punch bag
- [ ] A man wearing sunglasses
- [ ] Someone wearing pyjamas
- [ ] A sumo wrestler
- [ ] A man wearing headphones
- [ ] A skipping rope
- [ ] A red scarf

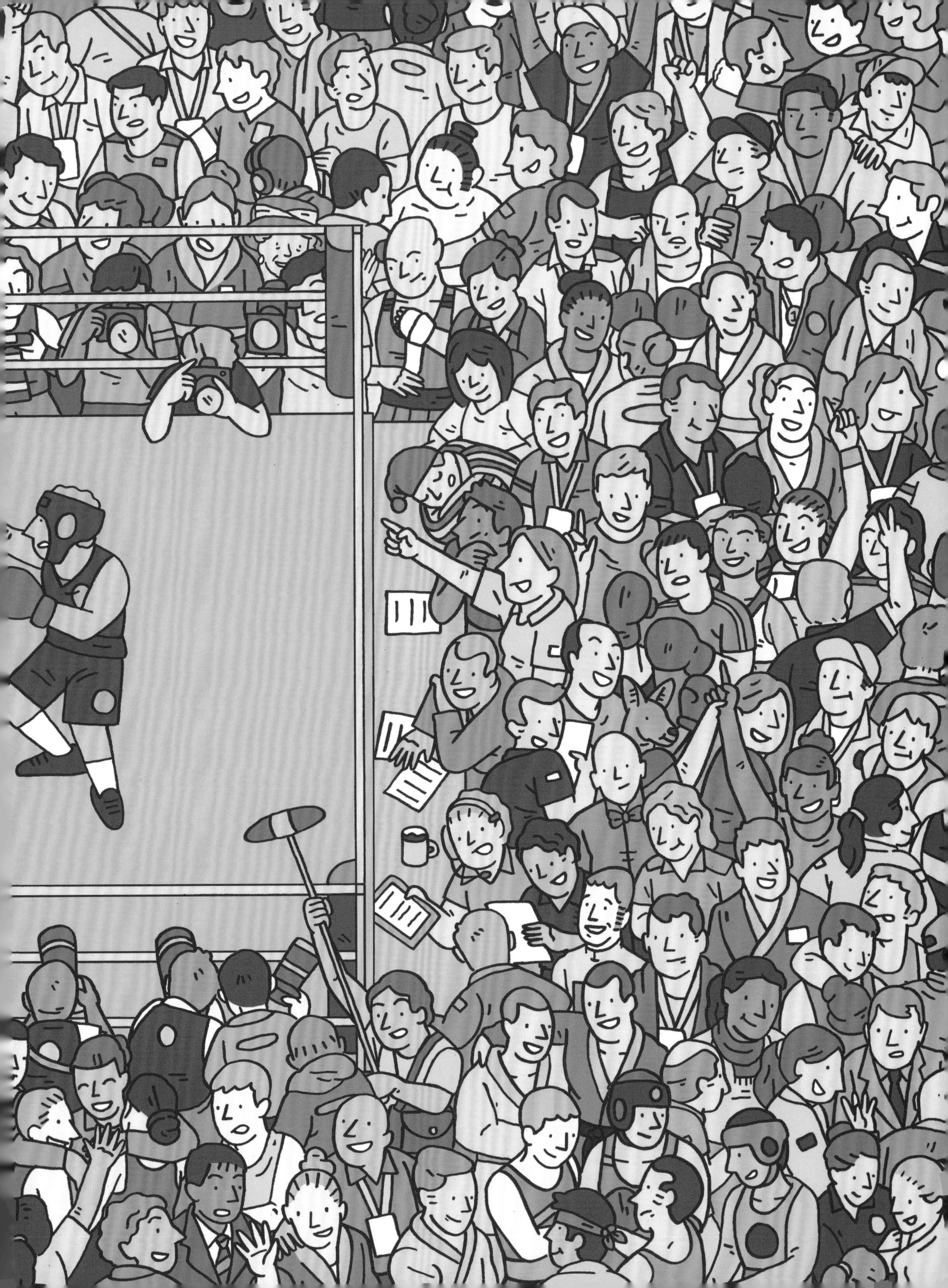

TRIATHLON

Wow! There are so many events taking place at the moment, Mo and his friends have decided to split up so they can cheer on all the athletes taking part in the triathlon. Can you find them to see which event they are watching?

Fun fact: The triathlon was only made an Olympic sport in 2000. The origins of the sport are unclear but the first modern triathlon took place in 1974.

CHECKLIST

- [ ] A duck
- [ ] A toy robot
- [ ] A squirrel
- [ ] A swimmer wearing an orange cap
- [ ] A gold bike
- [ ] A mermaid
- [ ] A garden gnome
- [ ] A rose bush
- [ ] Someone eating a burger
- [ ] A man rowing a boat

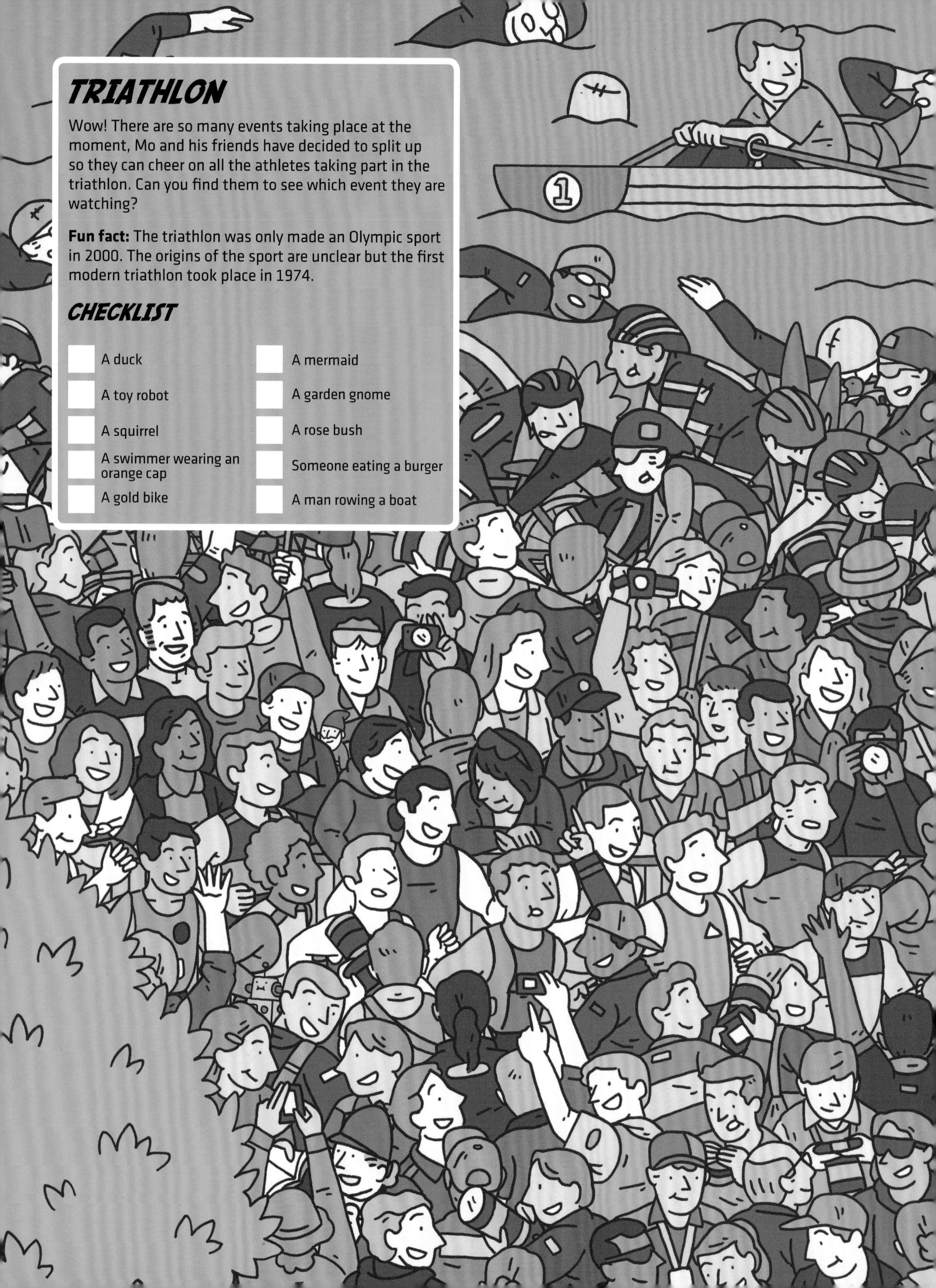
1

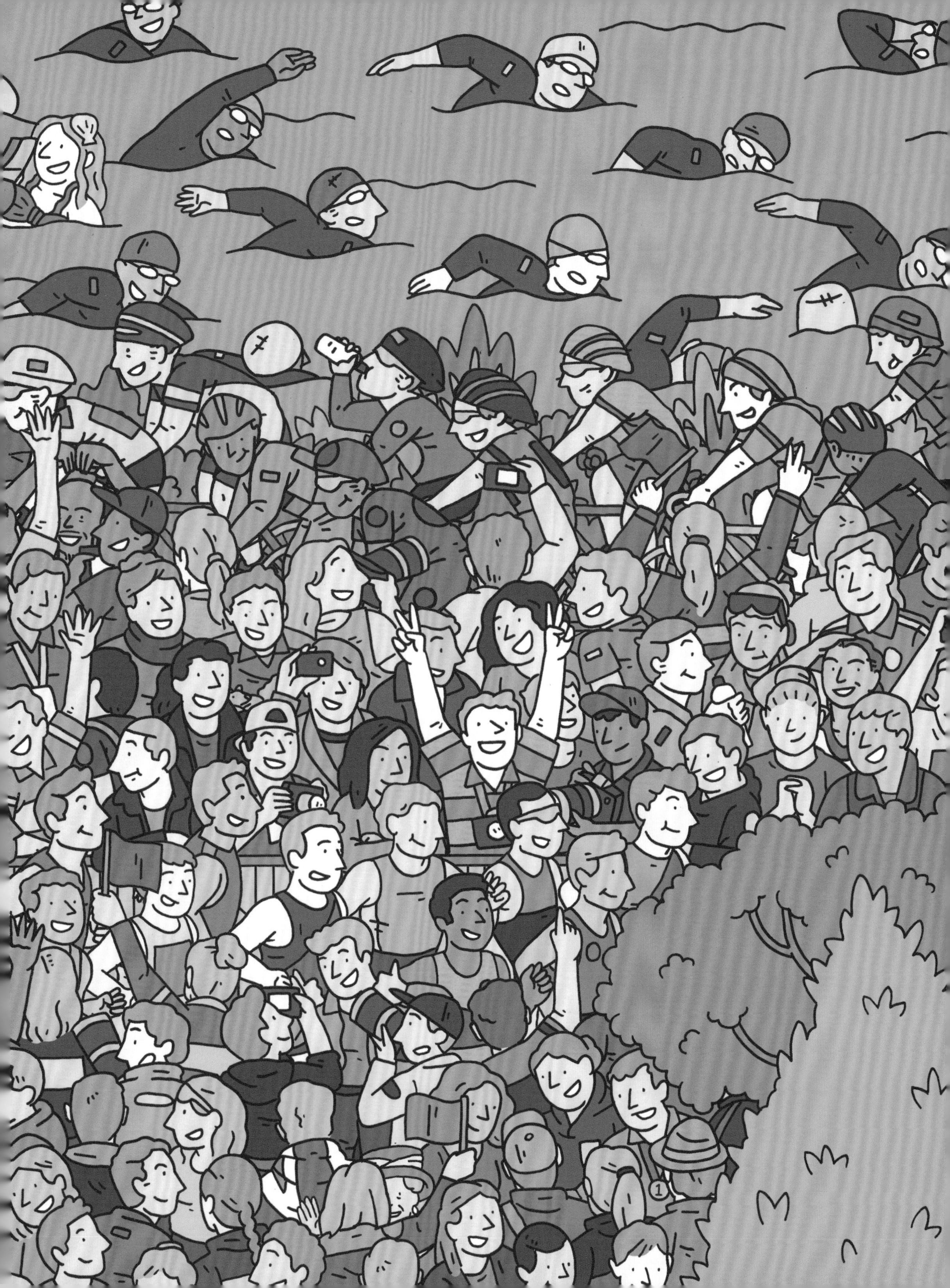

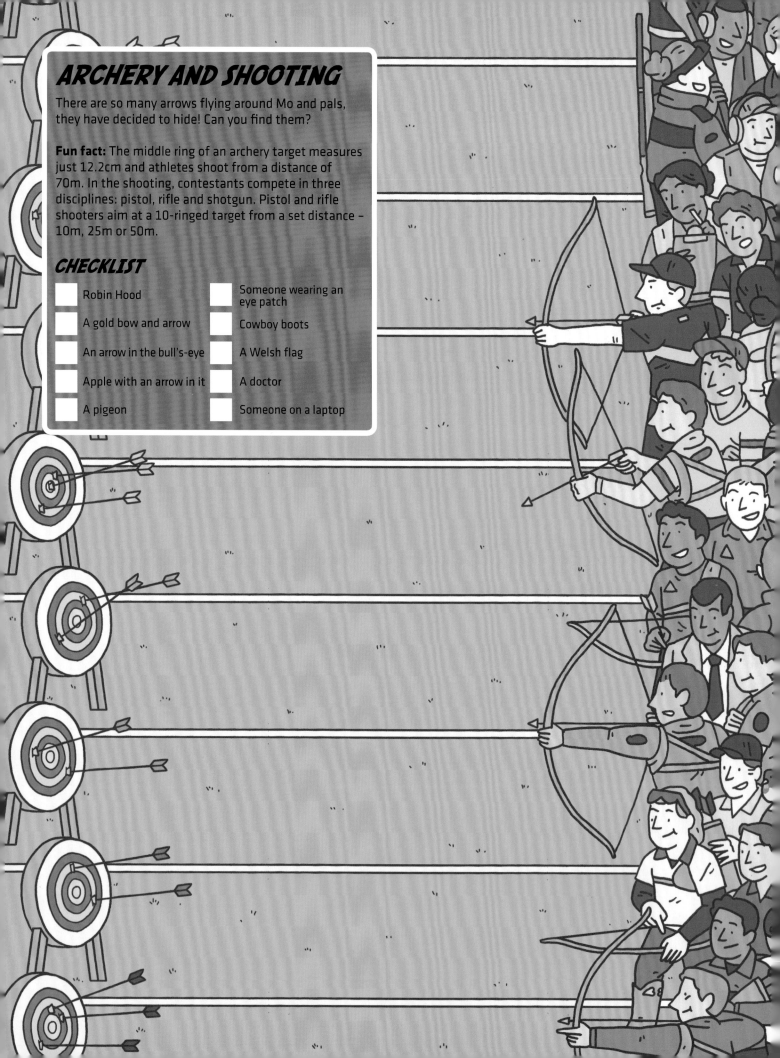

ARCHERY AND SHOOTING

There are so many arrows flying around Mo and pals, they have decided to hide! Can you find them?

Fun fact: The middle ring of an archery target measures just 12.2cm and athletes shoot from a distance of 70m. In the shooting, contestants compete in three disciplines: pistol, rifle and shotgun. Pistol and rifle shooters aim at a 10-ringed target from a set distance – 10m, 25m or 50m.

CHECKLIST

- [ ] Robin Hood
- [ ] A gold bow and arrow
- [ ] An arrow in the bull's-eye
- [ ] Apple with an arrow in it
- [ ] A pigeon
- [ ] Someone wearing an eye patch
- [ ] Cowboy boots
- [ ] A Welsh flag
- [ ] A doctor
- [ ] Someone on a laptop

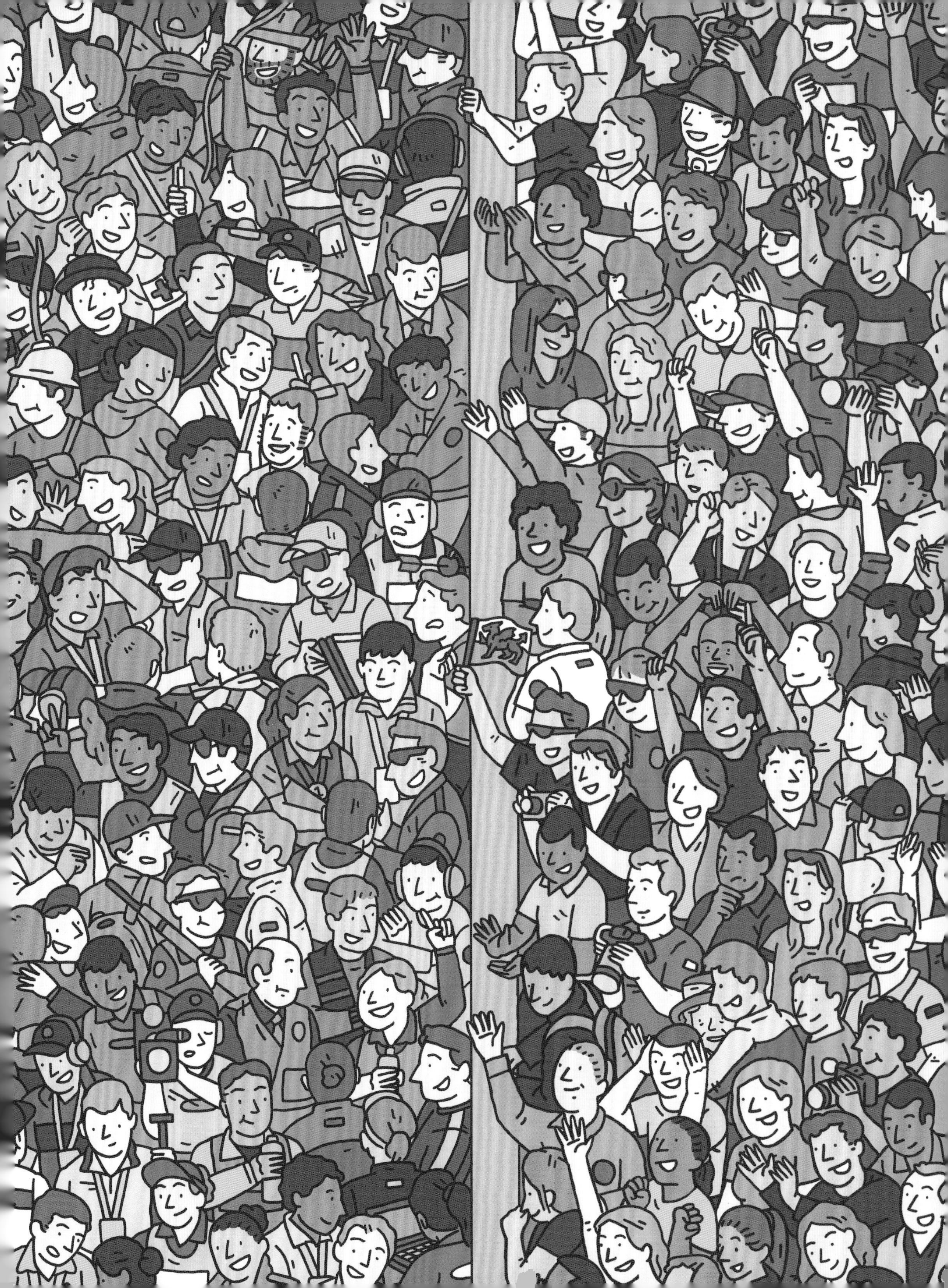

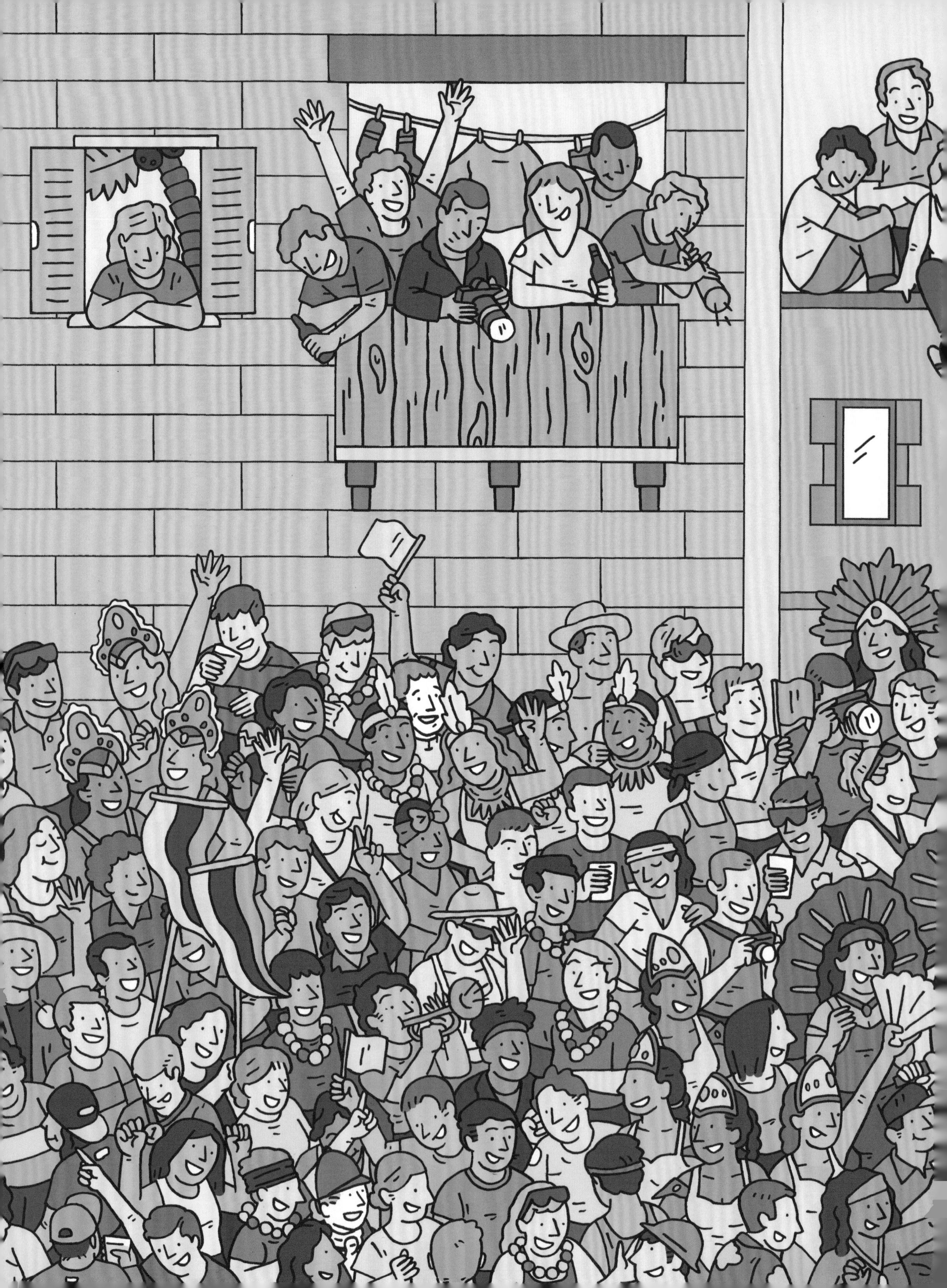

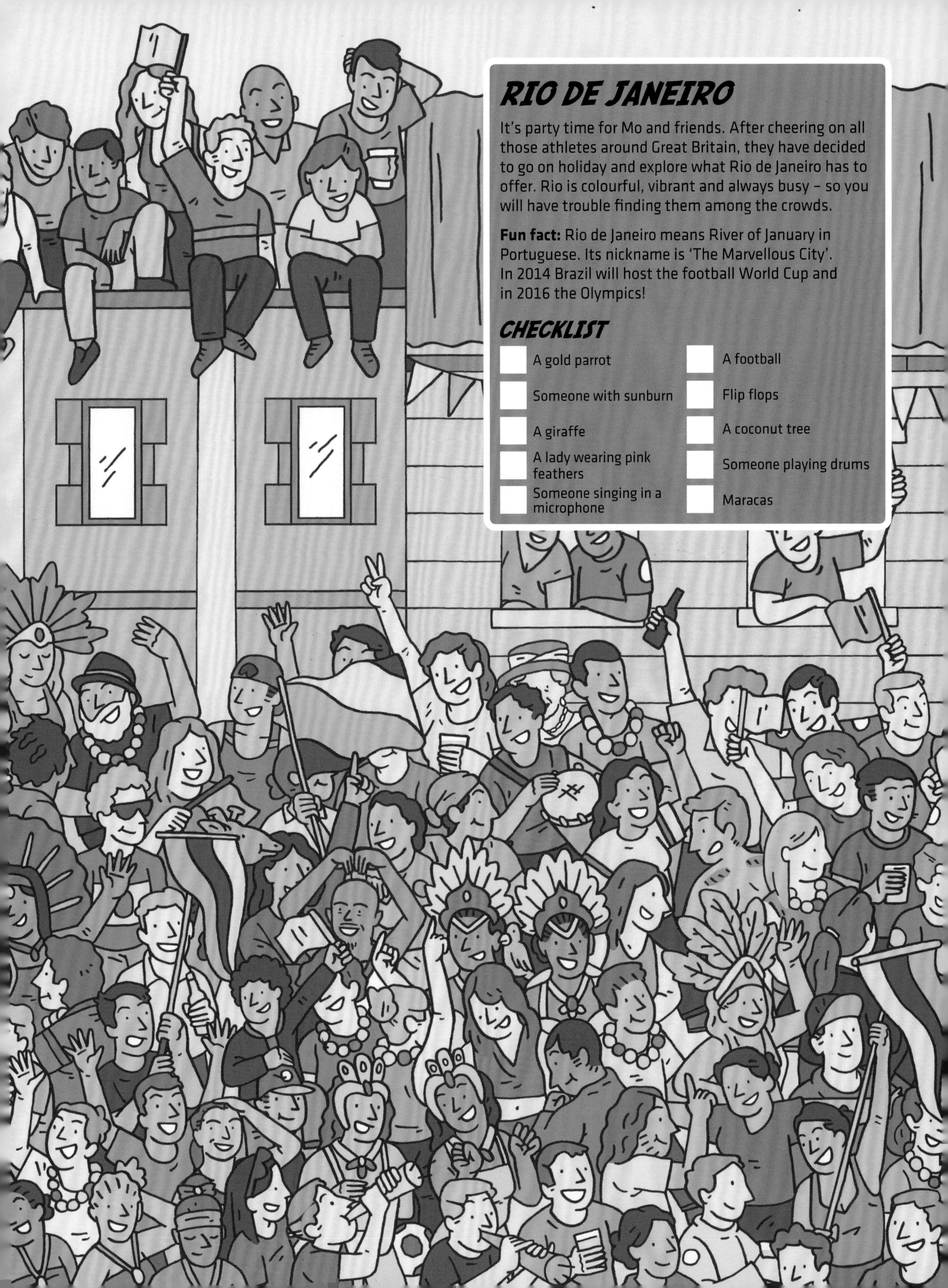

RIO DE JANEIRO

It's party time for Mo and friends. After cheering on all those athletes around Great Britain, they have decided to go on holiday and explore what Rio de Janeiro has to offer. Rio is colourful, vibrant and always busy – so you will have trouble finding them among the crowds.

Fun fact: Rio de Janeiro means River of January in Portuguese. Its nickname is 'The Marvellous City'. In 2014 Brazil will host the football World Cup and in 2016 the Olympics!

CHECKLIST

- A gold parrot
- Someone with sunburn
- A giraffe
- A lady wearing pink feathers
- Someone singing in a microphone
- A football
- Flip flops
- A coconut tree
- Someone playing drums
- Maracas

MO, MO, MO

It's time to head home after partying hard in Rio. How many Mos can you find in this picture?

☐ Add them up and put your answers here.

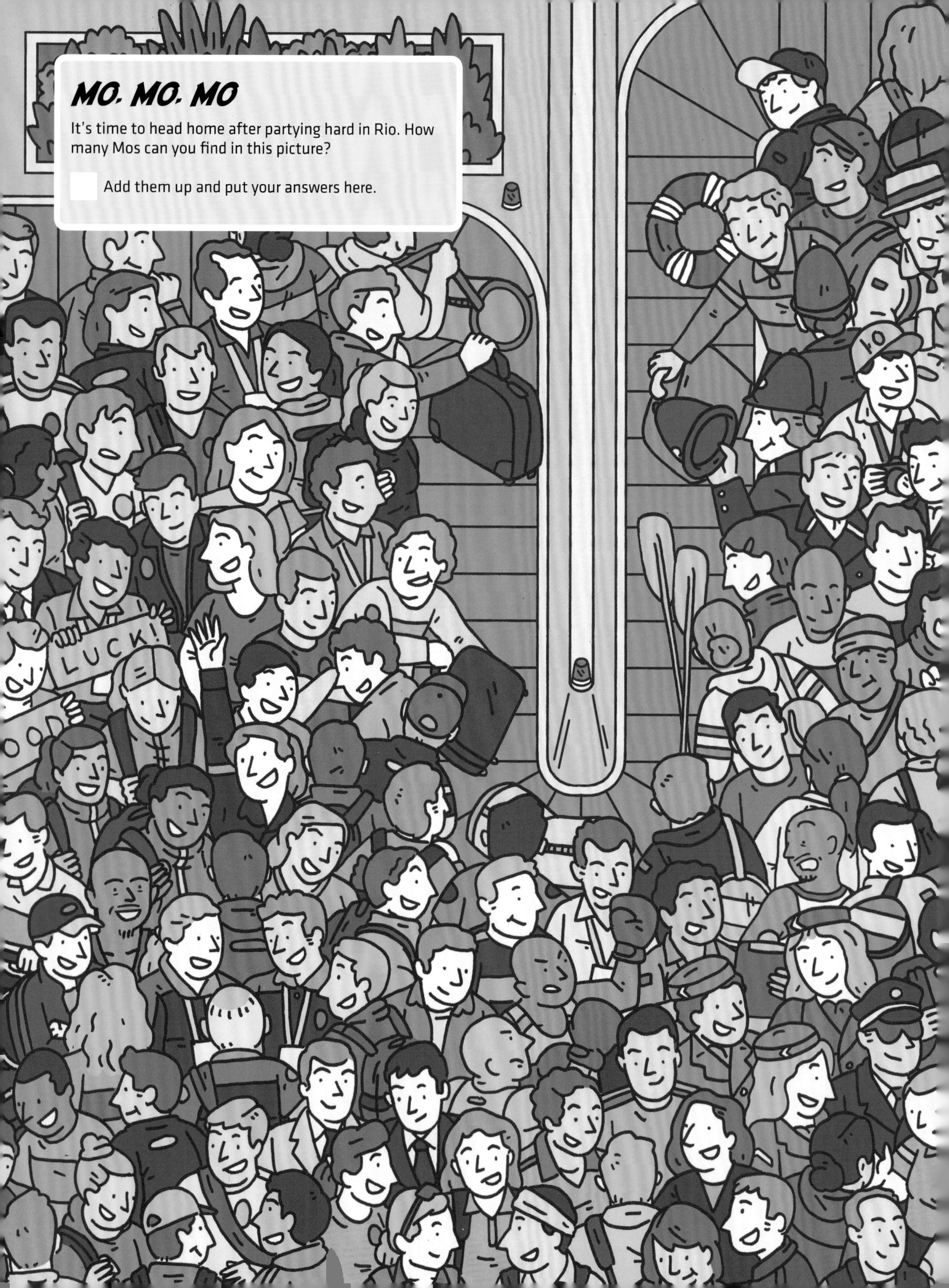
LUCK!

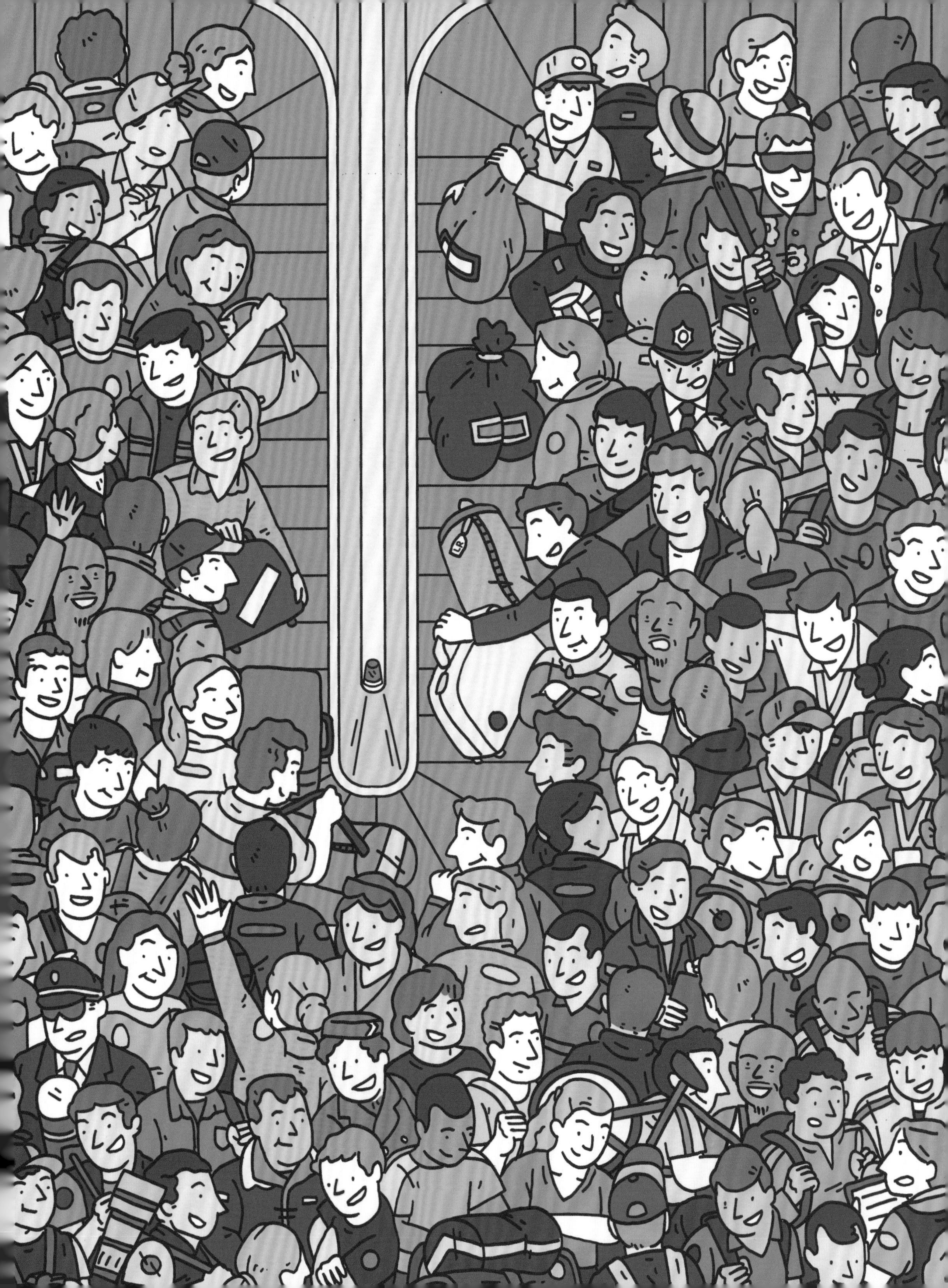
LR

ANSWERS

Did you spot the Queen? She has been hiding in 14 of the events. Go back through the illustrations to look for her... she's wearing a blue hat! If you can't find her, she is circled in the answers below.

TRACK STADIUM

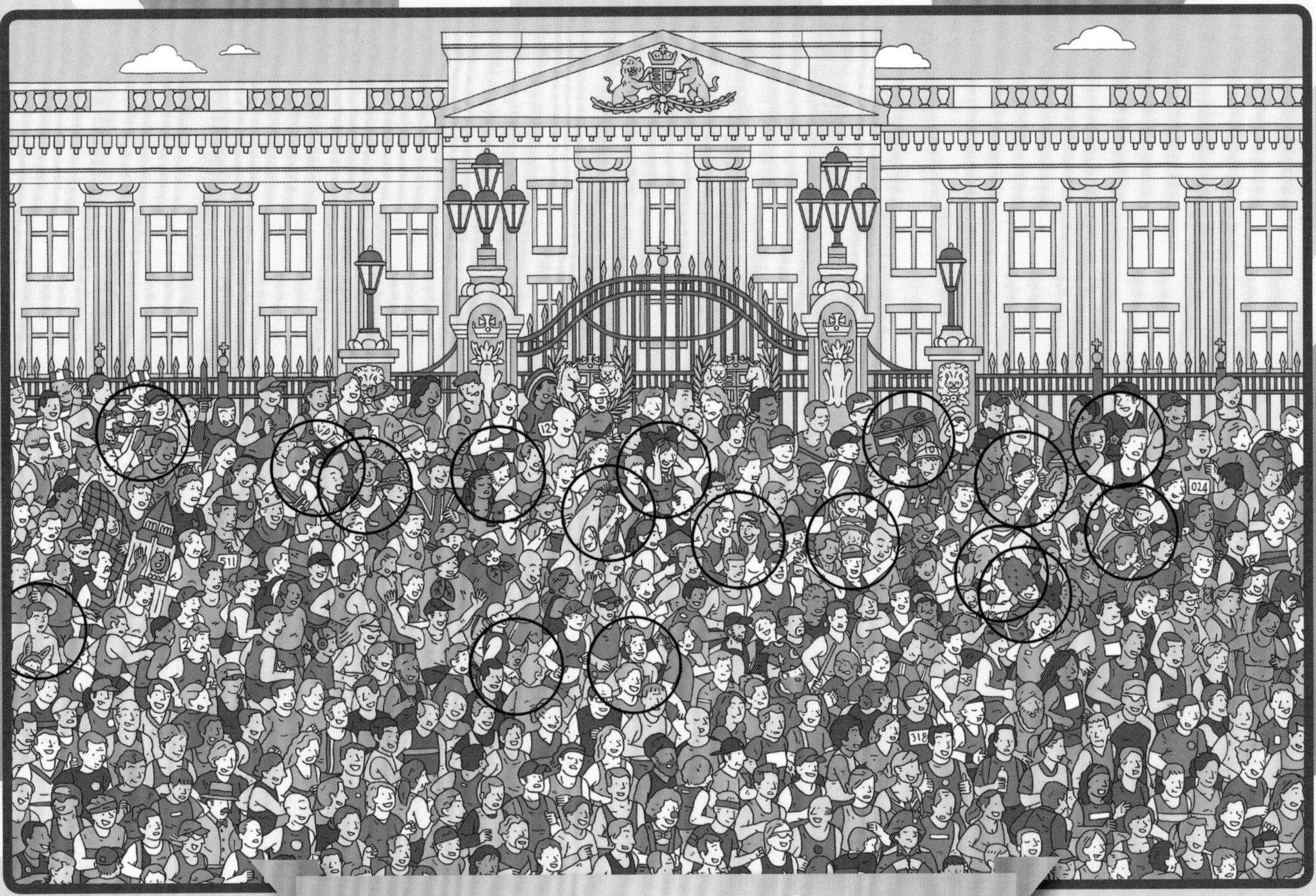

LONDON MARATHON

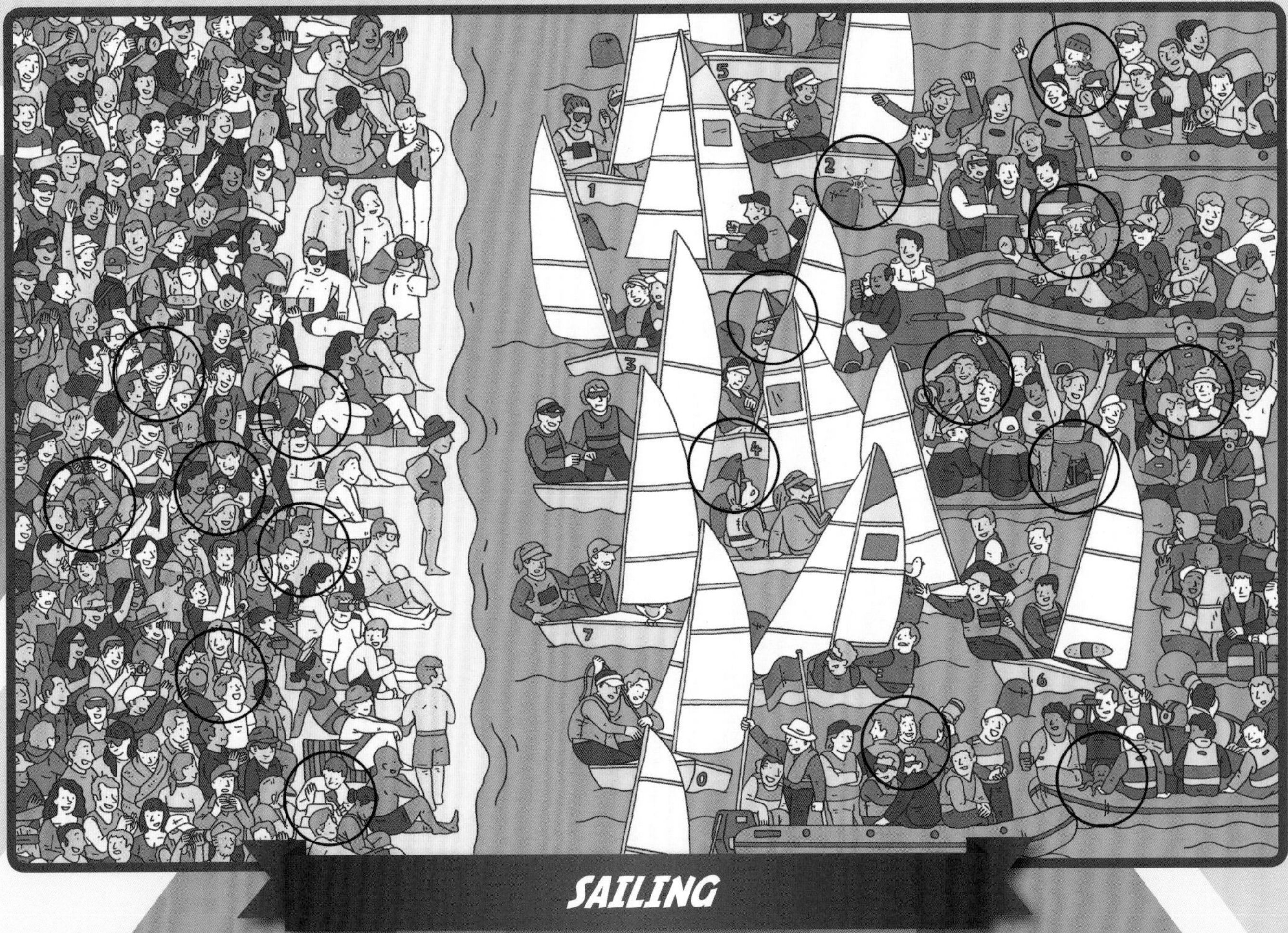

SAILING

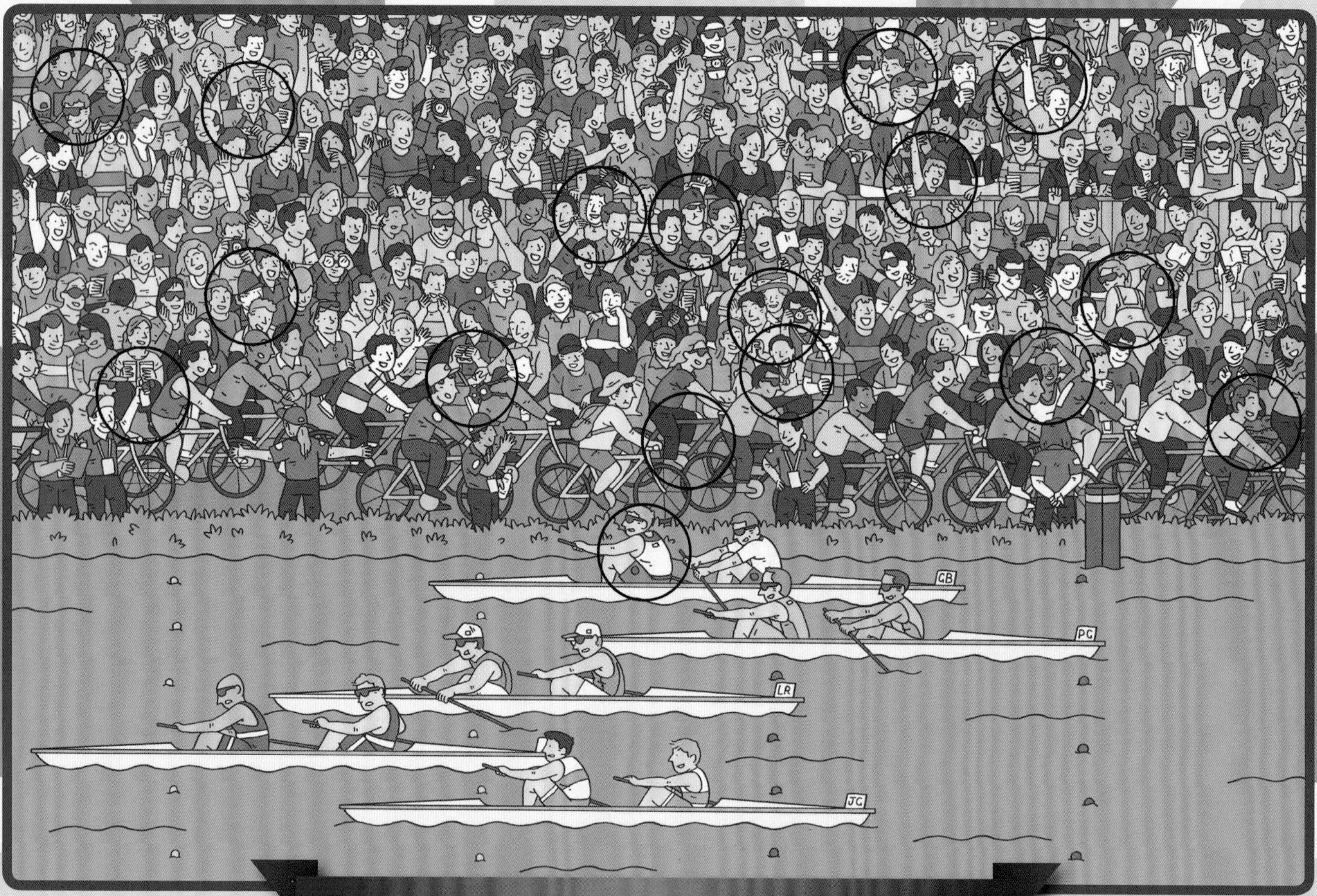
GB
PC
LR
JG

ROWING

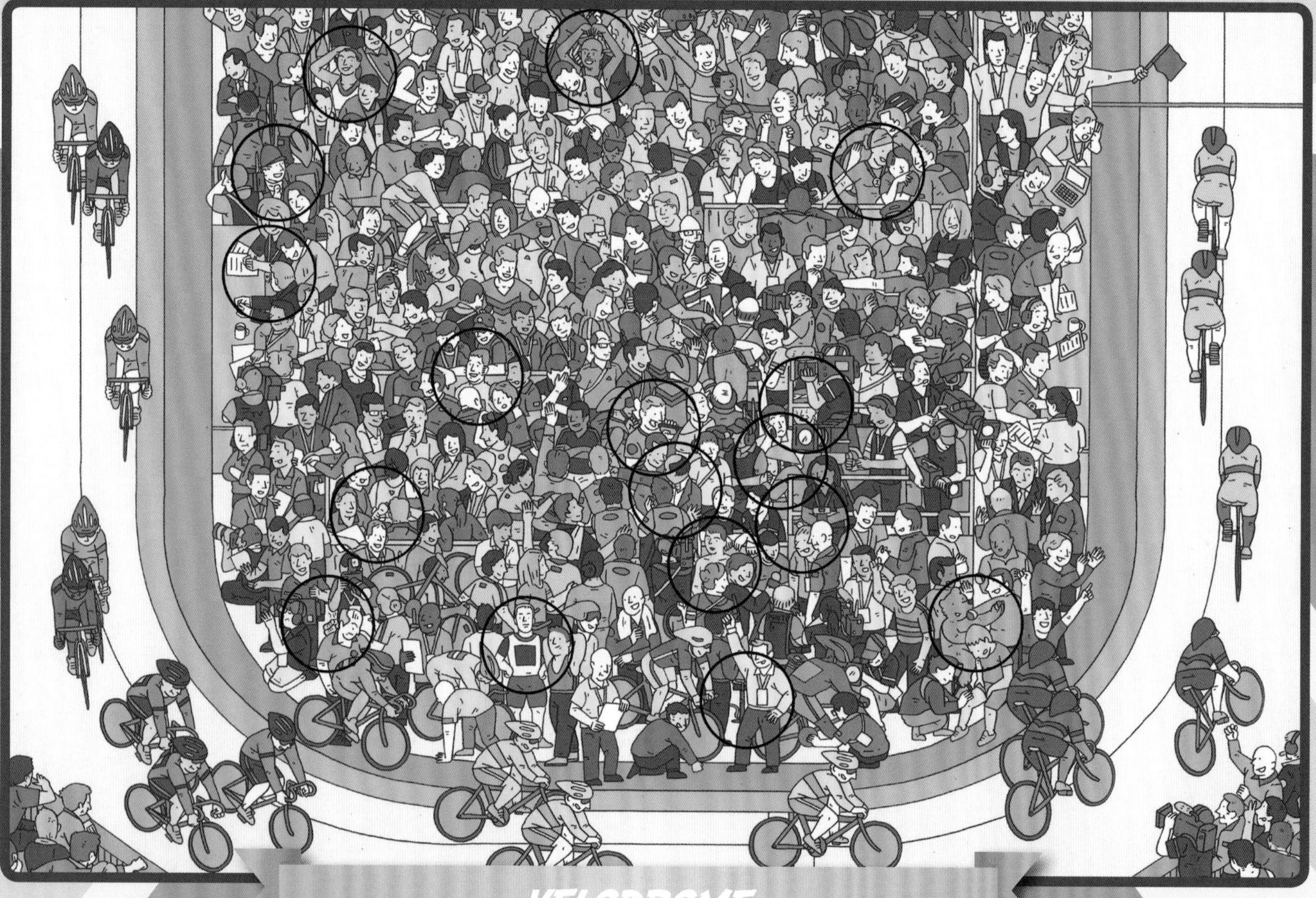

VELODROME

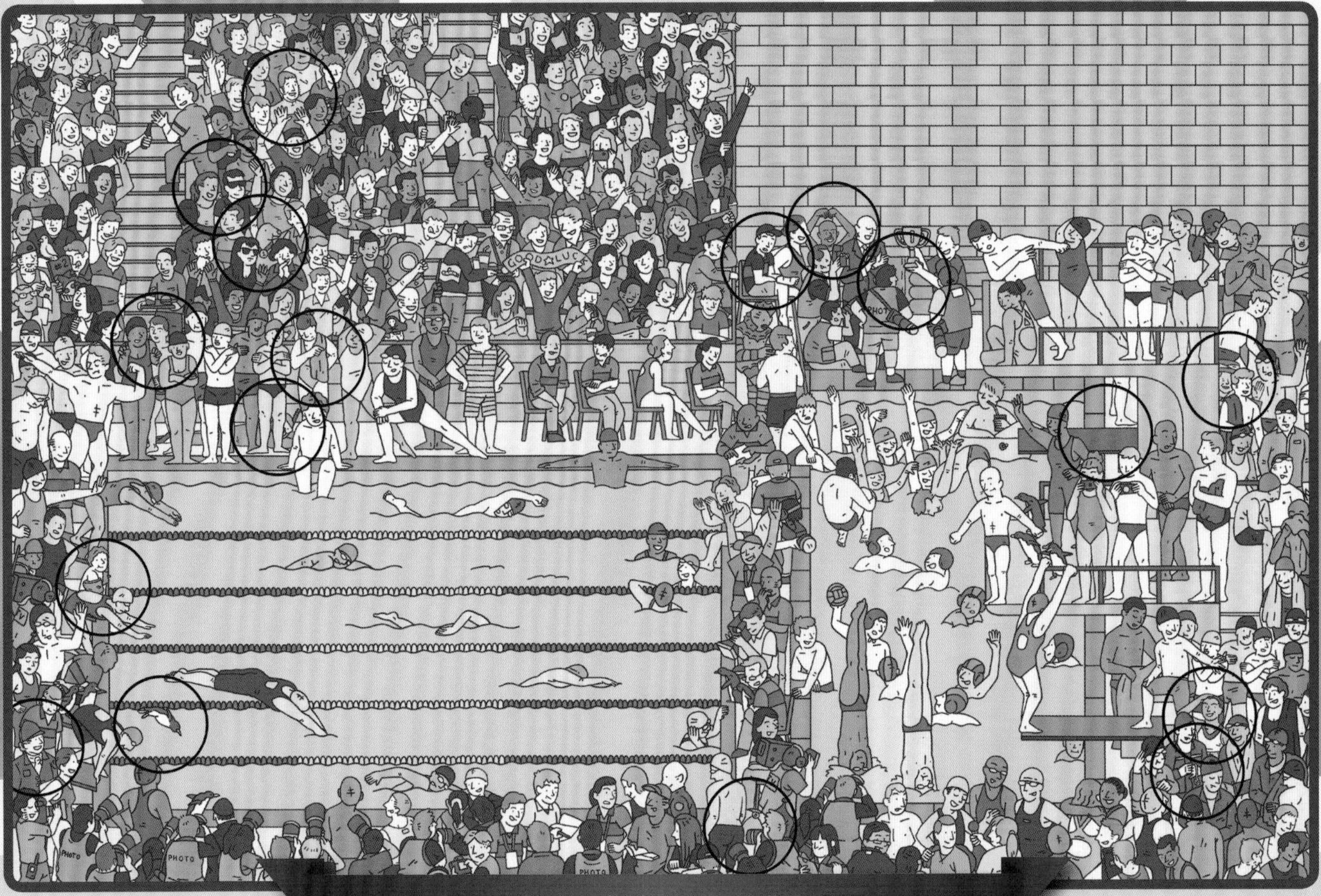
PHOTO
PHOTO

SWIMMING POOL

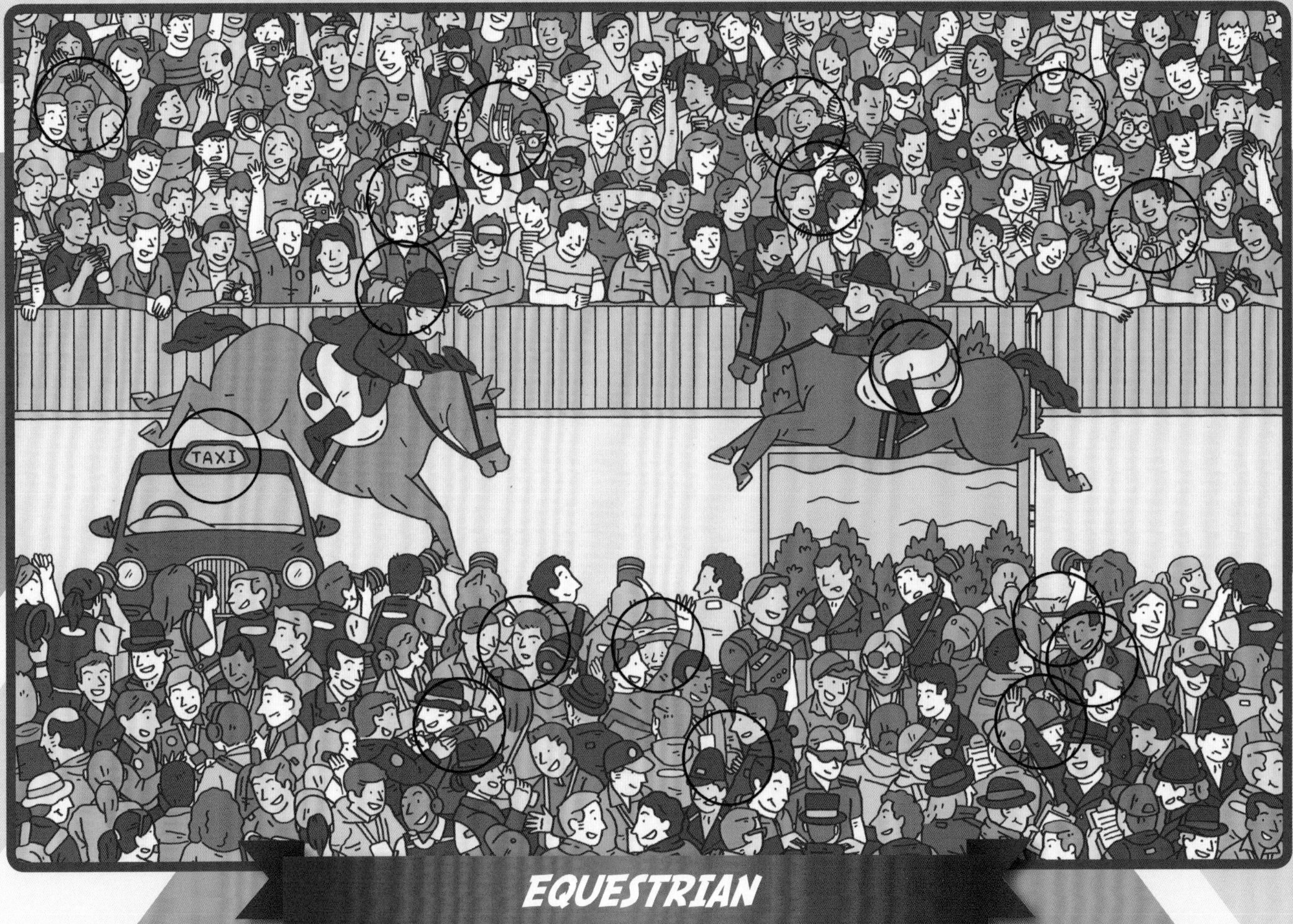
TAXI

EQUESTRIAN

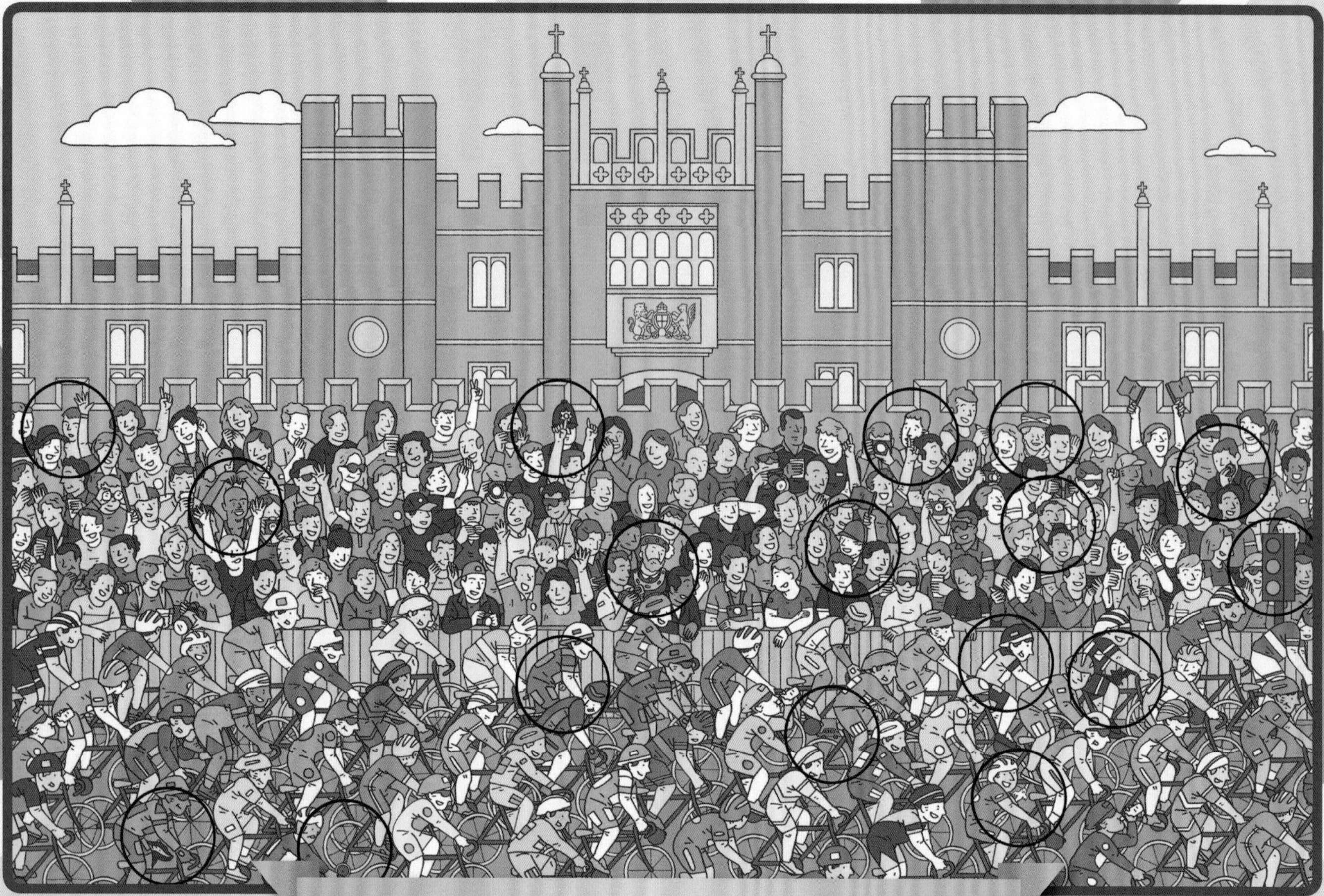

CYCLE ROAD RACE

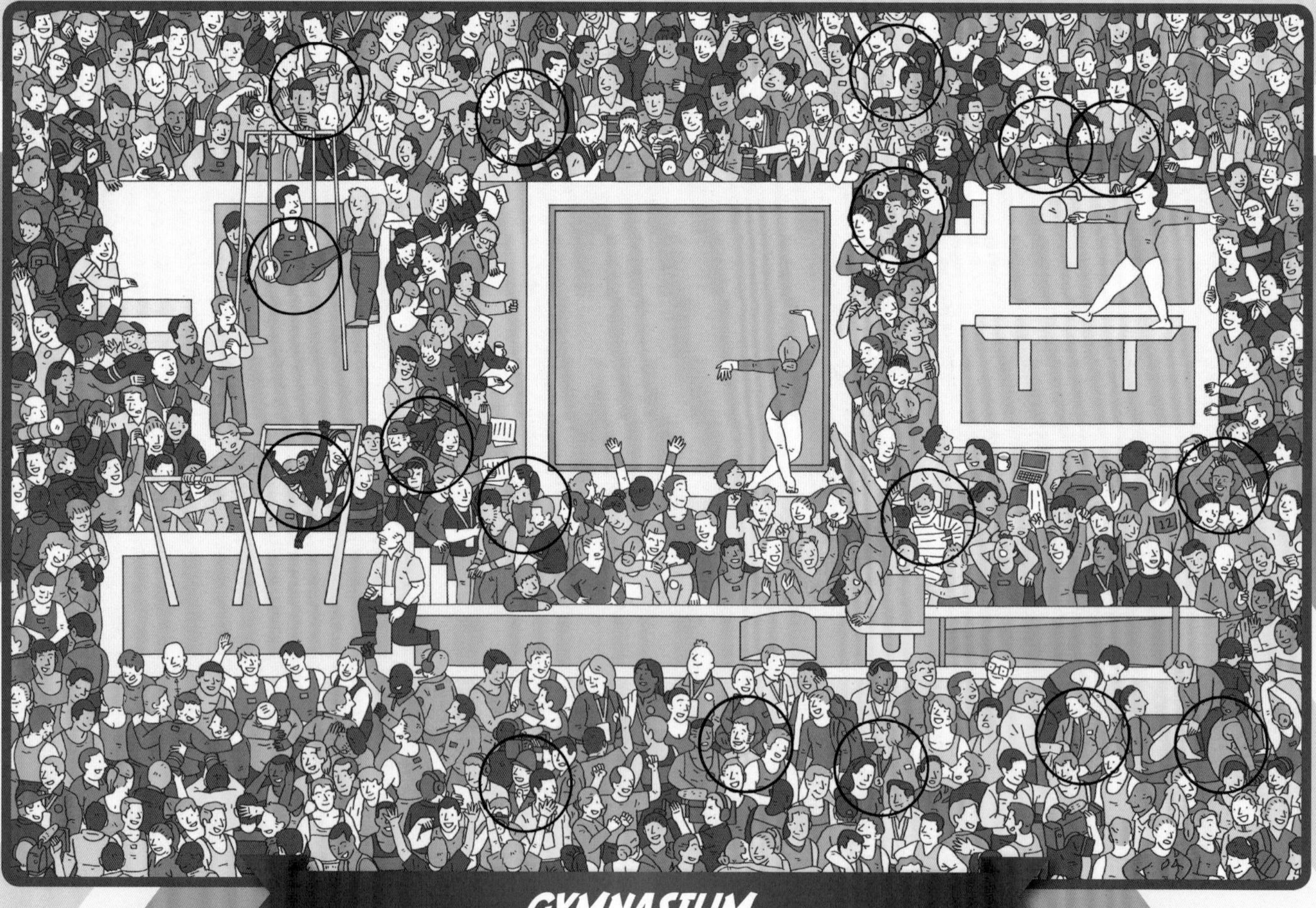

GYMNASIUM

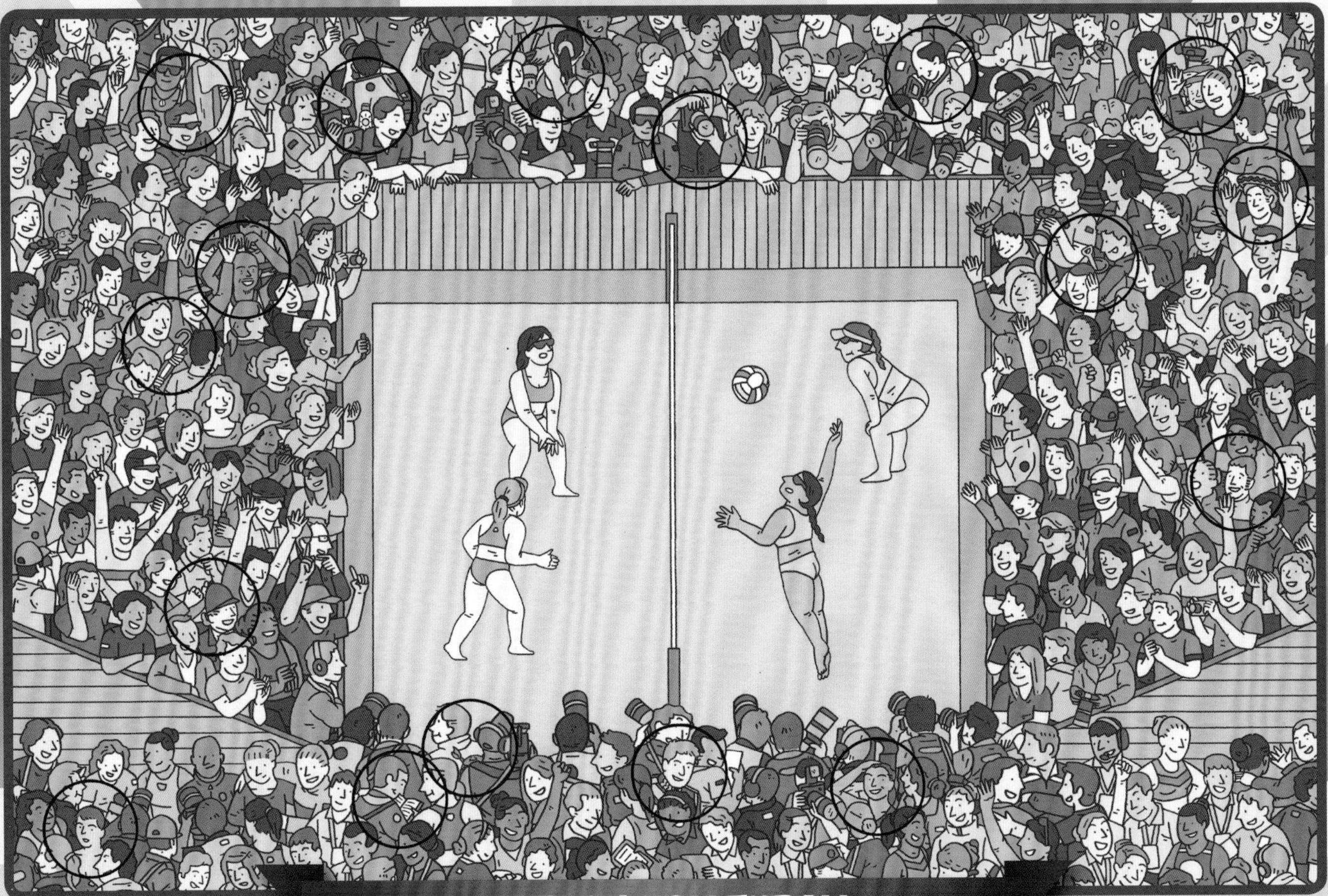

BEACH VOLLEYBALL

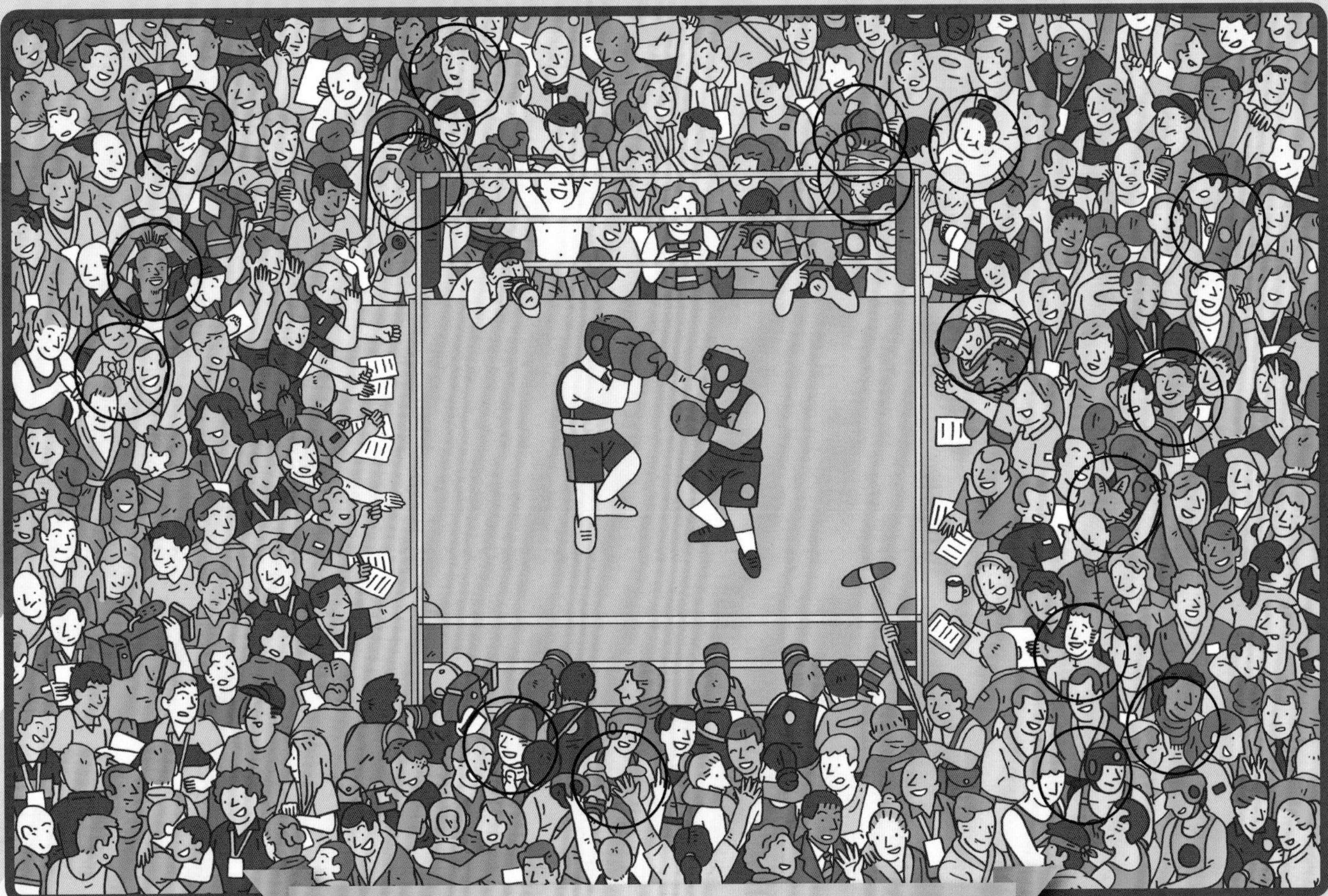

JUDO AND BOXING

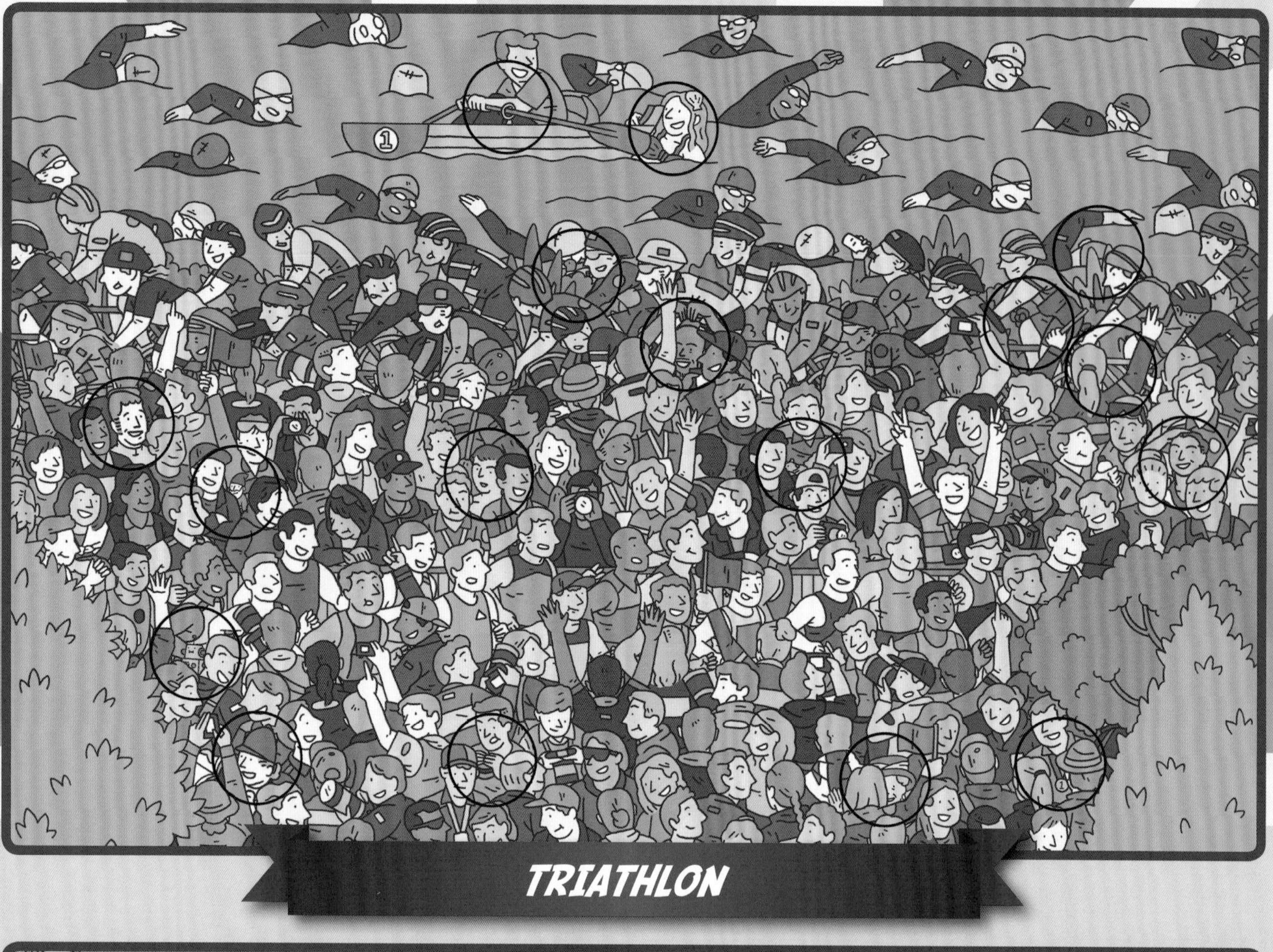

TRIATHLON

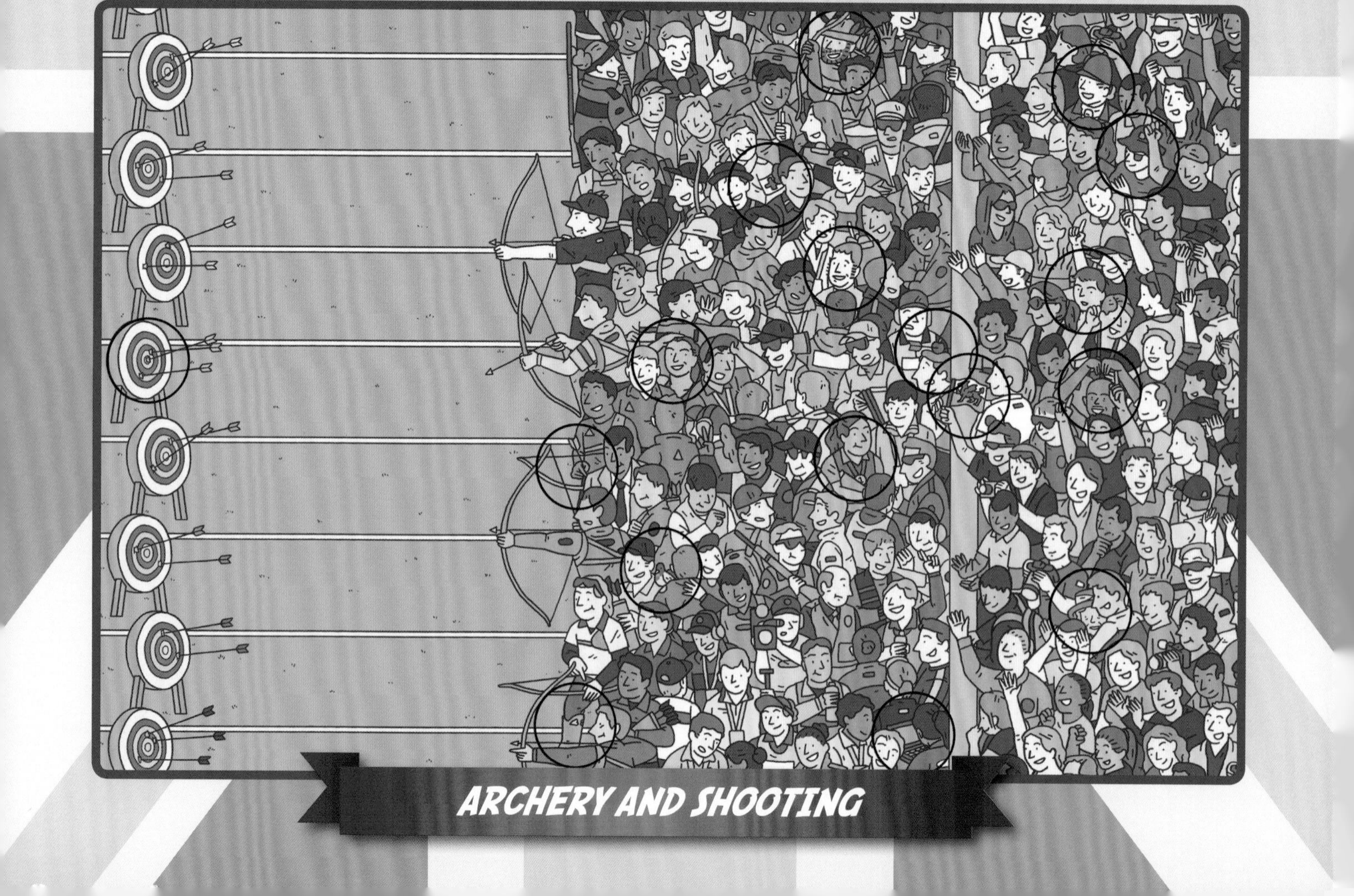

ARCHERY AND SHOOTING

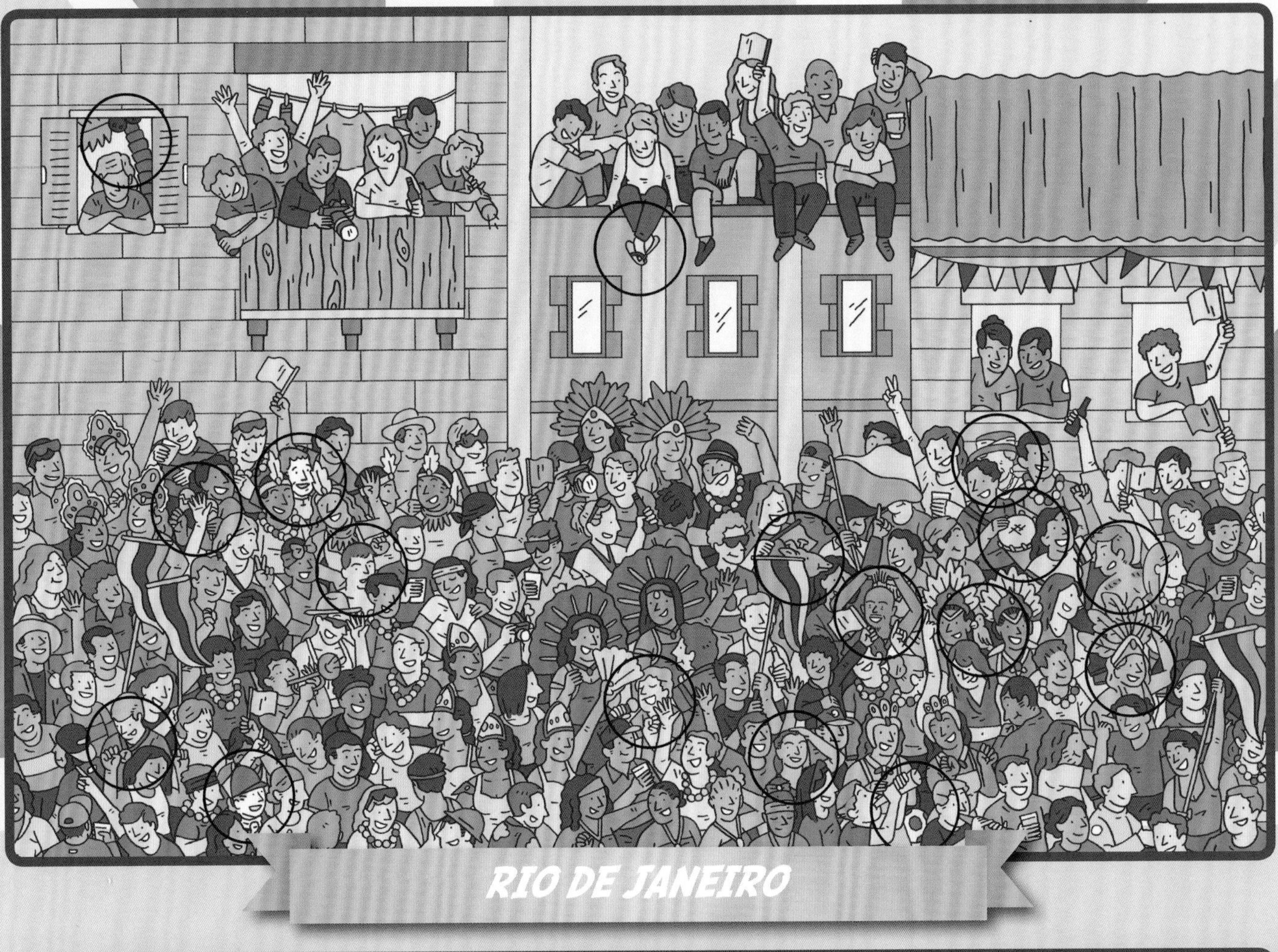

RIO DE JANEIRO

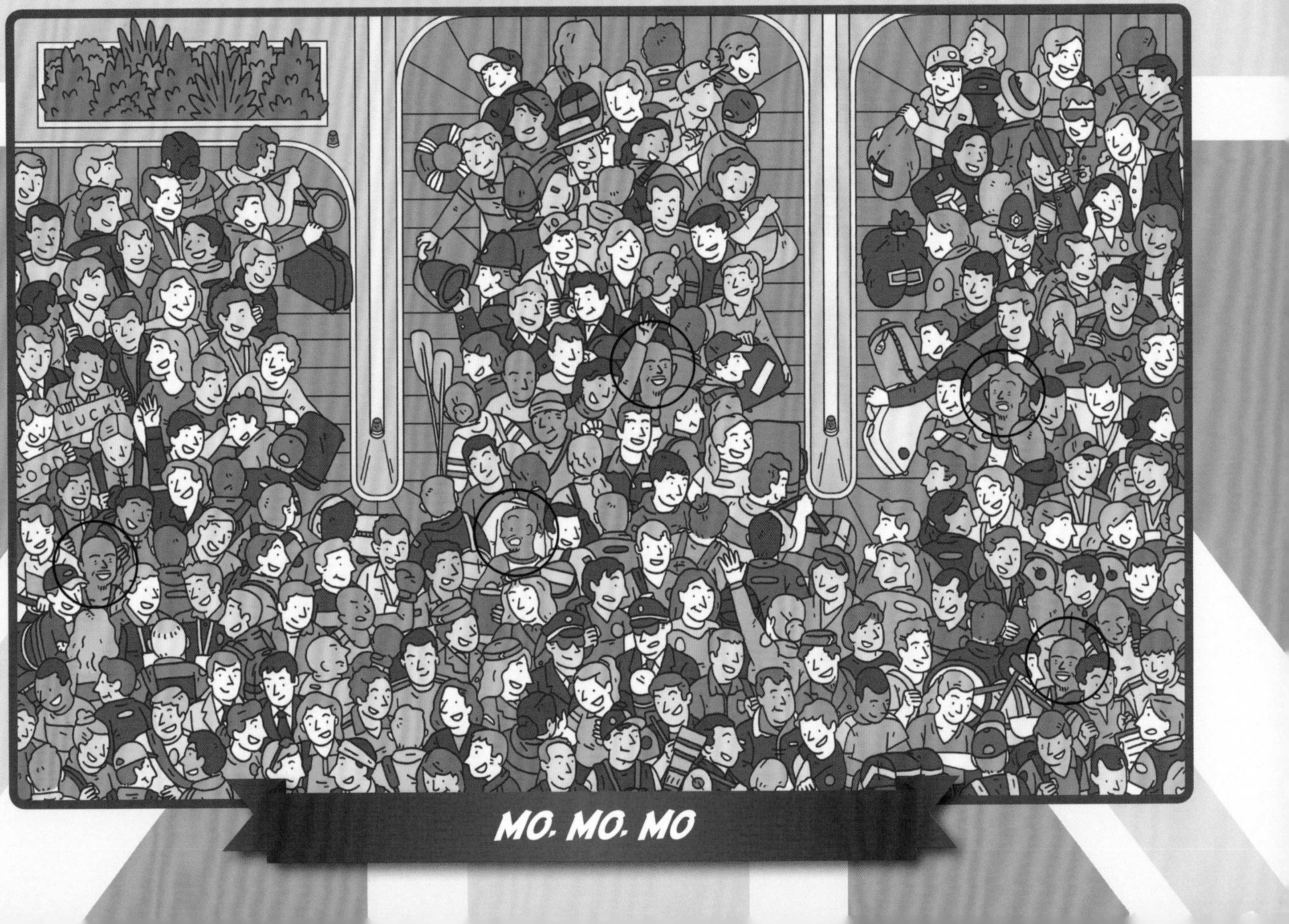
LUCK

MO. MO. MO

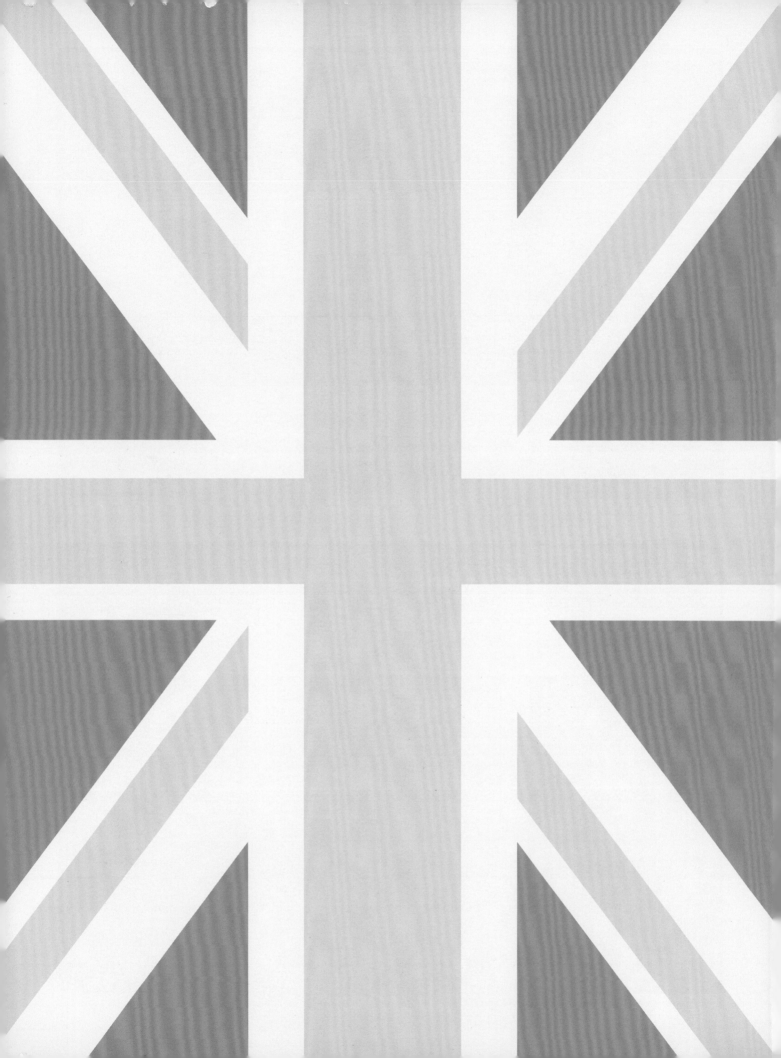